Omna Berick-Aharony, PhD

Producer & International Distributor
eBookPro Publishing
www.ebook-pro.com

THE HABIT OF HAPPY
Omna Berick-Aharony, PhD

Translation: Grace Michaeli
Contact: omna10@gmail.com

ISBN 9798875546006

THE
HABIT
OF
HAPPY

99 *Practical Lessons on Finding,*
Achieving, and Maintaining Happiness

OMNA BERICK-AHARONY, PhD

This book is dedicated to my brothers
David and Yehonatan,
who were lovely and pleasant
in their lives and in their death.

Contents

Acknowledgments

Anyone who ever had to submit an assignment at school, you very well know that writing is a lonely art, yet it requires tremendous support from the people around you. This is even more so if you're writing an entire book. Me, I'm a lucky woman, and I have an amazing and supportive environment. So this is a good time to express my gratitude.

First and foremost, thank you to my mother, Rachel Berick, who taught me to think and observe the world, and to my father Zvi Berick, who taught me that words are emotions.

Thank you to Meytal Bar Zohar, who made me mark down a specific date, and by doing so, helped me make a dream come true.

Thank you to Carmel Kerman who guided me like a devoted doula until I birthed this book. And to Tomer Kerman, who dotted all my i's and crossed my t's.

A big thank you to Elul Aharony, my sweet daughter, who was patient and handled all the challenges I threw her way, and illustrated this book.

I would also like to thank my children, Rotem, Ofer, Noam and Yuval, who listened, answered, read, and responded.

Thank you to all my beta readers, who took the time to give me feedback and comments that have improved everyone's reading experience.

And a great thank you goes out to my beloved Odi, who always inspires me in his own loving and unique way.

How Did I Become

a Happiness Researcher

How Did I Become a Happiness Researcher?

Worrying is What I Do Best!

I'm the absolute best at finding or making up reasons for why things could go wrong, get off track, lead to an accident, or a catastrophe. And yet, I never anticipated my beloved brother's advanced cancer diagnosis. I never anticipated that we would all be utterly helpless and unable to do anything to save him. Even the wildest, most anxious scene produced in my mind couldn't have imagined such a scenario.

My name is Omna and about a decade ago my life had completely changed.

We lived in Melbourne, Australia back then, which is the most pleasant place on earth. The Australians refer to it as "down under." We lived in a pleasant neighborhood, I studied at a pleasant university, and we shopped at a pleasant grocery store; life was a Hallmark moment.

We weren't planning on living in Melbourne forever. Not even close. We chose to live there for a while and teach our four children that life can be experienced in many ways: from down under, for instance.

Every couple of months, my dear husband Odi would

fly back home for his job. In March 2006, Odi went back home to fly the airplanes and their passengers to their spring holidays. He was away for a month and a half. I missed him for a month and a half, and I spent the time with my four children, ages sixteen to two-years-old, parenting as a single mom in a foreign land. It was the longest month and a half in my life.

A Low Blow
And then, one day, at the end of April, Odi returned to Melbourne. After the initial excitement wore off, he spoke to me in private and told me that my older brother, Dedi, had cancer. It was a low blow because as I had previously mentioned, I wasn't expecting such a disaster.

We packed our entire life into a couple of suitcases as quickly as we could, we carried everything with us on an airplane, and returned to our homeland. Then started a painful and hard period in our lives, during which we were all committed to alleviating my dear brother's pain and processing the daunting fact that we would soon have to say goodbye. After a matter of three months, my older and beloved brother passed away. It was a terrible loss for us all, and all I did for a whole year was cry.

Everything that I did throughout that year was affected by the pain of that loss. However, I wasn't afraid of the pain. I realized that the pain was from now on a part of me, and if I tried to deny it or ignore it, it would only hurt more. Furthermore, during that period of time, I recognized a couple of very meaningful things. First, I grasped the immense power that pain has when we simply let it be. I didn't try to hold my tears back; I felt that I needed to unload that immeasurable pain, and crying was a wonderful outlet. When people would unknowingly ask how I was doing, they would immediately see my eyes well up and hear a true story about pain and grief.

A couple of years passed, and I still felt that I was in the worst place I had been in my entire life. On paper, I had everything a person could ask for: a good relationship, perfect kids, a comfortable home, and an interesting job that I was also good at. I had also successfully completed my PhD. Yet something deep down was morose, bored, and dissatisfied.

After that painful loss, I felt that Dedi's passing shook me beyond the sadness and sorrow brought on by his death. I felt as if life itself had become gloomy and quite gray.

One morning, I said to Odi: "I don't know what to do anymore! I'm simply unhappy!"

My wise, beloved man looked at me and replied: "My love, our life is as sweet as a bowl of cherries. You have me, the great love we share, and we have wonderful children. We live in our dream house and we both love our jobs and earn enough to live comfortably. What you're going through cannot be changed from the outside. It's time that you look inward and find what can make you happy from within." So, I took his advice and decided to examine what would make me happy in that sad routine of mine.

Revelation: Happiness Cannot be Outsourced

And thus began a journey. A journey to discover my inner happiness. On this journey I realized that happiness cannot be outsourced; it's a practice that needs to happen inwardly. It was a long and complex process, leaving no stone unturned inside of me. I willingly peeked into my darkest corners, I uncovered various pains and the ways I processed them; and having done all that I paved my path of happiness. I read research on what empowers our happiness and I took a course on happiness at an American university. I practiced a variety of methods that help people reach happiness, such as meditation, mindfulness, happiness exercises, practicing gratitude, forgiveness, and reducing self-criticism. That being said, a personal reflection didn't suffice. Through my own research – both personal and professional – and hundreds of hours in my clinic, I developed a new and unique way to reach personal happiness.

Seeing as I am a psychotherapist with more than thirty years of experience, the most natural way to begin applying this method was during my sessions with my own clients at my clinic. Those sessions in fact brightened my sadness a little, because I sensed how much I had helped my clients. You could even say that this pain sharpened my professional skills. I could understand my clients' pain on a deeper level; I was unafraid to touch their most deeply-seated and agonizing wounds. We fearlessly spoke about death, diseases, anger, and aches. Of course, the research instruments I had studied and developed throughout my PhD were the perfect toolbox for such inner explorations.

My PhD is in gender studies and it examines the impact of the geopolitical conflict – in which Israel has existed for nearly a century – on models of femininity within Israeli society. This research has allowed me to create methods through which I can examine reality from a different perspective, and uncover how social and personal beliefs affect our worldview and even some of the most common daily behaviors, such as choosing what to wear every morning. Yes, even day-to-day and simple fashion is affected by our thoughts and innermost beliefs. So naturally, these tools assisted me in fully comprehending how we can create our own reality through our thoughts, and how this reality affects the way we feel in our day-to-day lives.

Later, I read hundreds of studies and tracked down the methods that according to all studies worked. I started teaching my clients these methods. I created exercises that would teach people how to reconnect and hear their inner voice after having ignored it for decades. I've picked up some techniques proven to be effective in research, and I've developed them, adapting them for easy and daily use.

A Simple Thank You

One of the amazing tools I discovered, for example, was gratitude journaling. It's a simple, accessible, and daily exercise of writing down five things that happened that day and made you feel grateful. Like any other exercise, I first tried it myself. Some of my friends and I established an online group, where we would write down and share every evening at least five good things that happened to us, and we expressed these things in a thankful manner. For instance:

"I'm grateful that I had enough milk in the morning

to make my coffee and I didn't have to leave the house without my regular hot beverage. I'm grateful that I easily found a parking spot this morning and made it to my meeting on time. I'm grateful for the flat tire I had on my way back home, because thanks to that I had a long conversation with my son and discovered a challenge he was facing at school. Tomorrow I'll talk to the teacher and resolve the issue. I'm grateful for having warm water and a pleasant shower. I'm grateful for my soft and comfy bed and for the beautiful and soft sheets I had received as a gift for the holidays from my mother."

Sounds fairly simple, but you wouldn't believe how this exercise can make a huge difference. Some studies have shown that practicing gratitude can help those suffering from depression overcome it. I know after years of practicing this exercise, both by myself and with my clients, that this small and simple act helped us retrieve our optimism and focus on the good things and be grateful for them. Focusing on the good is the name of the game. This tool also works if we write down what we're grateful for in a personal notebook. However, gratitude becomes a powerful tool if we open a group on some digital platform, such as social media, and share our gratitude list with others.

As I drafted the outline for the sessions and exercises, I began to realize there was an entire method at play, a method I would like to teach in order to help others increase happiness in their lives. So, I founded **The HappinesSkool**. I started teaching courses which explained in depth the meaning of the portals to happiness and the perception that happiness is an internal journey that depends on our perception of reality. I taught my students important tools and exercises that would assist those who learned the method to boost happiness in their lives as well as cope with pain and challenges. As I dove deeper and expanded the method, I realized that I wanted to pass along the method to everyone. My next step was to open a Facebook page for **The HappinesSkool.** I began giving online lectures and live sessions to the public. The lectures were about coping with pain and struggles, and how we can increase happiness in our lives.

The realization that happiness benefits our general health and not only our quality of life drove me to spread my method even wider through my courses. During the two-year pandemic, as the whole world battled the Coronavirus and faced the accompanying health and daily challenges, I gave online lectures and wrote on every media platform at my disposal, on how to expand happiness in times of hardship. To this day, people call me out of the blue to thank me for my teachings.

Currently, some people simply refer to me as Dr. Happiness. I guess you can even say that because of the profound pain I had experienced, my perception of life and the world and how we all handle our lives has completely transformed. Thanks to this pain, I was compelled to look inwardly, find my inner happiness, and truly understand the source of my joy. After conducting extensive research and hundreds of sessions in my clinic, examining what invokes happiness in people, and investigating how we can create and increase happiness in our day-to-day lives, I've developed the Seven Portals model.

I spread this method through **the HappinesSkool** that I have founded.

Here it Comes Again

In October 2020, in the midst of the Covid-19 pandemic when we were all still afraid of the virus, I received a phone call. It was during a holiday, early in the morning, and the house was very quiet.

"Omna?" I heard my young brother Yehonatan's voice on the other side of the phone. "Is this a good time?"

"Yes, I'm at home, Jonny, what's going on?"

"Are you alone?"

I assumed that he wanted to talk to me about something private. So I simply replied that I wasn't on my own, but I'll go somewhere quiet.

"Sit down," he replied.

Now he had my attention.

"What's wrong, Yehonatan?" I asked.

"I'm at the hospital. I had a CT and they found a tumor in my abdomen. We don't know a lot right now, but I didn't want you to be on your own when I told you."

Someone in my head screamed, *No, this isn't happening*.

But the holiday morning silence still engulfed me.

Then, I embarked on a journey.

On a geographical journey, I tried to reach Canada where my brother had lived for the past thirty years. I set out on this journey in the midst of a pandemic, when the world had gone completely out of its mind – closing its borders and requiring special permits. It was also an emotional journey during which both my mother and I stayed optimistic and hopeful – a hope that only three weeks later would be shattered when we had to send him off on his final journey. The journey was also an internal one; I negotiated with myself, with the universe, and with anyone who would lend an ear, the terms of maintaining happiness, even when faced with a massive crisis and incomprehensible pain.

Yehonatan passed away thirteen years and one month after Dedi, our older brother, passed away. I'm writing these words during the days between Dedi and Yehonatan's memorials. Some people refer to this period as "the Holidays," yet I refer to it as "between memorials." With the holiday festivities, of joyous and loving family gatherings on the one hand, and the grief and sadness of having lost both of my brothers on the other; I find myself compelled to muster heaps of awareness every year, making sure to keep anger, self-pity, and pain at bay. Every year I use the Seven Portals, and a myriad of insights I have collected and shared here with you, in order to stay happy and spread the word of daily and tangible happiness to whoever wants to learn. The years since Yehonatan passed were my test run. Would the Seven Portals assist me in overcoming the pain a second time around? I believe that the portals have proven themselves over and over again.

Almost two years after Yehonatan passed away, his children were finally permitted to travel to Israel. It had been two years since we last hugged them in Ottawa and left with my little brother, my mother's youngest son, their father, whose coffin was stored in the plane's cargo.

Due to the COVID-19 lockdowns and living in terror, they were refused a travel permit to the funeral and memorial, even though they had asked multiple times. They arrived with their dear mother after almost two years. We could finally hug them, cry, laugh, talk, and eat together!

It was their first time visiting their father's grave, even though they witnessed the funeral and first memorial via a video call. That visit was the first time they had physically been to his grave. My heart pounded in my chest. All I wanted to do was hug them and make sure they knew how much we love them and how we all missed Yehonatan.

Life is riddled with challenges; loss, diseases, grief. No one can live life pain-free. That moment, as I see it, is a wonderous combination of love and pain, joy, and sadness. I did my very best to focus on the joyful aspect of that moment, the great love we shared, and our love for Yehonatan. I allowed the tears to roll down my cheeks, and knew that this was all a part of life; and this too shall pass.

So, Why Portals?

Happiness isn't a goal.
Happiness isn't a diploma
to hang on the wall.
Happiness is a voyage!

So, Why Portals?

Seven portals that assist us in realizing our place on our journey of happiness

Half a century ago, we had hundreds of psychological studies about anger, and not even a single study about gratitude. We had thousands of studies about why couples divorce, and no studies about the makings of a good marriage. There were countless studies about anxiety, and not even one about compassion. Studies examining the downsides of Cortisol and stress hormones, but almost none that examined the factors of well-being. For more than a century, modern psychology focused on researching the human soul, resulting in most of the research revolving around the reasons behind anger, the damages brought on by anger, why we're anxious, and the physiological effects of anxiety.[1] The purpose was to alleviate and reduce the pain of those who struggled with depression or anxiety.

Around the end of the 20th century, a new paradigm within the discipline of psychology started to develop, called positive psychology. This doctrine stated that

1. Seligman, Martin EP, and Mihaly Csikszentmihalyi. "Positive psychology: An introduction." Flow and the foundations of positive psychology. Springer, Dordrecht, 2014. 279-298.

while it's important to treat depressed people and elevate them on the scale of happiness from a minus five to a one, it is also important to help people move on from a level two to a level six and be pleased and happy with their lives. Thus, psychologists started researching questions such as: What is happiness? What are its components and factors? How important is happiness for our physical and mental health? How can it be increased? Over the course of fifty years, the concept of well-being became the subject of psychological research, and we've gained plenty of information on the causes of happiness and on the factors that impact our level of happiness. The first dilemma researchers faced was how to measure happiness. Or perhaps more accurately, how could happiness be defined?

A Process; Not a Goal

Happiness is perceived differently in different cultures. However, we're gradually discovering that happiness is a process, not a goal. Due to extensive research about well-being and happiness, we now have plenty of information about how we can help ourselves live happier lives. Myriad articles and books about the happy brain and the obstacles on our path of happiness have been written. Researchers have also found a formula that tests the extent to which happiness is hereditary; that is, dependent on our genetics, and the extent to which our lives' circumstances, otherwise referred to as 'luck,' affect the degrees of happiness that we have or can potentially reach.

I often compare the great volume of information

collected about happiness to a large table covered in disorganized papers, all piled up. Very few outstanding individuals know this material so well that they can approach that heap of documents, reach out, and quickly pull out the piece of information they're after. But most of us do not have the access, ability, or knowledge necessary to make use of this information. Therefore, we're unable to use this rich source to produce effective methods that can have an impact on our levels of happiness.

An Organizer of Happiness

This is where I come in. Over the past few years, I've organized a method, or rather an organizer. This organizer has seven compartments in which I have arranged the information about happiness that has been gathered throughout the last decades. The information is out there; I did not create it. However, it's been piling up in disarray, making it hard to realize the potential that lies within. Now, with my method of the Seven Portals of Happiness, this information is available and applicable.

Why Do I Call Them Portals?

Well, as I've previously mentioned, happiness isn't a goal. Happiness isn't some diploma to be hung on the wall. Happiness is a voyage!

Picture a camel train crossing the desert. The blistering sun shines down on them, and water is scarce and precious. The camels are laden with spices and perfumes, and the cameleers are tanned and scrawny. Their heads are wrapped in thin scarves, sheltering them from the sandy breeze, and their long *galabias* protect their already-sun-kissed skin. They aren't pacing down a marked road, and the fact that they know where they're headed may be incomprehensible to a foreigner. The desert seems to be uncharted territory, and the train's path is long and arduous.

This is young Aretas' first journey down the Incense Trade Route. He nervously looks around him; it's been two days since they last saw a milestone marking the right path. He was beginning to worry. He turns to his father and asks him: "Father, how do you know this is the right path? How can we tell if we took a wrong turn?"

His father's face is riddled with coarse wrinkles and his skin is dry and brown; his entire head is wrapped in a shawl, but from between the folds of the delicate white fabric, two green eyes peek at Aretas. He squints, and Aretas can imagine his father's familiar smile, slowly spreading underneath the white fabric. The father doesn't say a word. All he does is point ahead, slightly to the right. At first, Aretas doesn't quite understand what his father is pointing at. However, as he tries to focus his gaze on that spot, he sees something large that appears to resemble a stone structure. As they approach it, Aretas realizes that it's a huge gate, a portal to the Nabataean city, Mamshit.

Of course, Aretas and his father are figments of my imagination, yet their expedition down the Incense Trade Route is very real. Just a little over two thousand years ago, the famous Incense Trade Route passed through the Negev Desert. The Nabataeans traded their myrrh and frankincense throughout that route, from the

Gulf Emirates, through Yemen, Jordan, the Negev, and all the way to the Port of Gaza, Greece, and then Rome. Long before people ordered their products from Ali Express and ASOS, those camel caravans delivered the most luxurious goods, such as perfumes, silk, and precious gems, all the way from the East to the West.

The road wasn't easy, and it stretched through deserts and seas. The Nabataeans who traveled this path had to master their journey and guide their camels along the trying road, keeping them on the track marked by milestones and Nabatean cities such as Avdat, Haluza, and Mamshit. Each of these cities confirmed that the train was on the right path and served as a docking and loading station. They'd restock their provisions in each city, knowing they hadn't lost their path and were on course. They'd enter each of these cities through a large and impressive gate, some of which have withstood two thousand years and exist to this day. These gates or portals are my inspiration for the Seven Portals of Happiness model.

Happiness lies in our relationship with ourselves, with others, and with reality. The Seven Portals are a roadmap of how we should navigate those relationships. Each portal outlines the right way to behave in relationships in order for us to uncover the happiness that lies within relationships, rather than focus on the pain, sadness, or disappointments that lurk in those relationships too. Every portal is like an ancient gate, yet has a revolving door through which one can enter into happiness and continue on the voyage of happiness in their life. However, if we keep walking through that revolving door, it can eventually kick us out, preventing us from "entering" into happiness. These portals are very simple, which is why they have an element of magic about them. The greatness of this method lies in its simplicity.

The Dialogue Between the Portals

According to Eastern philosophies, the chi — life's energy — flows throughout our body through seven energy centers, known as "chakras," that manage our bodily energetic resources. The Seven Portals and seven energy centers correspond with one another; they converse with each other, but they aren't controlled by each other. We can agree that all the organs in our body are equally important (can we really choose which is more important; the liver or the pancreas?). Similarly, all the portals are significant; one is not more or less important than the others. Each has a certain significance in increasing our happiness, well-being, and wholeness. The portals are intertwined. For example, when I'm grateful, I'm aware of what exists in my life, which allows me to give freely. When I'm in a state of compassion, and I reduce judgment, I can accept the circumstances around me more easily.

Each and every one of us has portals that are stronger and those that need to be strengthened. The deeper we familiarize ourselves with these portals, the better we will be at communicating with one another and with our energy centers. This will eventually lead to a voyage of happiness as a way of life.

HOW TO READ THIS BOOK

The book is a 21st century philosophy book.

It contains 99 thoughts about happiness
and a few other mediations.

The book can be binged, like a show on Netflix,
or read in singular sections, like YouTube clips.

You can read about all the portals in the
order in which they were written or
a bite of a thought here and there.

In short, you can read however you like!

And Now

What Portals are
Your Strength

What Portals Are Your Strengths?

Questionnaire

Seven Portals on the Journey of Happiness

- What portal is wide open to you, and which do you have to work hard in order to go through?
- By answering this questionnaire that I have developed, you'll easily recognize your happiness level, strengths, and challenges.
- I recommend answering each question intuitively (all answers are correct and valid).
- Write 1 or 2 in the "answers" column based on the answer you've chosen.

The Habit of Happy – This is the time to begin

QUESTION	Answer number 1 or 2	Sum of the points of each portal
When I hear the word 'no' or when things don't happen my way, I: 1. Get upset and try to do everything I can in order for things to happen just the way I want them to. 2. I try to understand why things aren't happening my way, and look for other ways to find a solution.		**The Portal of Acceptance**
When I receive a present, the most important thing is: 1. Having a gift receipt, in case I want to exchange the present. 2. Someone thought about me, and wanted to make me happy.		
When I give a present, the most important thing is: 1. I've given what was expected of me, and my present is worthy and appreciated. 2. I make sure I have thought about the person receiving the present.		**The Portal of Giving**
When I see someone who's dressing well or someone who has done something great, I: 1. Wonder to myself whether they're better than me. 2. Love to compliment them and make them feel good.		
When someone has made a mistake, the most important thing is: 1. Explaining to them why it's a mistake, what they've done wrong, and where else they've made that mistake. 2. Helping them realize that we all make mistakes and it's a part of life.		**The Portal of Compassion**

If I've scheduled a meeting with someone and they're running late, I'll think: 1. Why is it so hard to be on time? 2. It can happen to anyone; we're only human.		
When I see a pretty flower or enjoy a delicious cookie: 1. It doesn't have any impact on me, it's just another part of life. 2. My heart swells with joy, and I feel very lucky.		**The Portal of Gratitude**
When something good happens to me or when someone helps me, I: 1. Believe that it's a given; this is the way things are meant to be. 2. Tell everyone, am thankful, and make sure to express it.		
When I'm sad, I tend to: 1. Remember and think about sad things that happened to me and others. 2. Allow myself to feel sad, but make sure not to lose myself in that feeling.		**The Portal of Joy**
When I watch TV, I'd rather watch: 1. News, scary dramas, TV series, exposes, or documentaries about injustices and corruption. 2. Funny TV shows, amusing video clips, science, or nature documentaries.		
When someone hurts my feelings I: 1. Will always hold it against them, think about it, and feel that life is unjust. 2. I won't think about it much. If necessary, I'll keep my distance so I won't get hurt again.		**The Portal of Forgiveness**

When I think about the mistakes my parents have made, it's clear to me that: 3. They've really screwed me over, and some things cannot be forgiven. 4. Every parent makes mistakes, and usually, they make those mistakes unintentionally and not because they don't love us.		
When I love someone, the most important thing is: 5. They think about me, they notice what I care about, and they give me attention. 6. To have fun together, do something together, and find things that we can enjoy together.		**The Portal of Love**
Love to me is: 7. A privilege that only some get to enjoy; it's often painful and makes me feel vulnerable. 8. The most important and therapeutic thing on this earth.		

Now, add up all the points in each portal separately.

Results

- 2 points for a certain portal –
  There's plenty to work on. You don't use this portal often in your life. However, by exercising it daily, it could become one of your happiness portals.
- 3 points for a certain portal –
  Great, this is a portal that can open the door to more happiness. Practicing can turn it into one of your strong portals.

- 4 points for a certain portal –
  Congratulations! This portal is one of your strengths
  on your path of happiness. This portal is dominant in
  your life and serves as an anchor to your daily journey
  of happiness.

Once you finish reading the book, I recommend taking
the questionnaire again. After all, the purpose of this
book is to balance every portal and make sure they work
in our favor.

What in Fact is

Happiness?

What in fact is Happiness?

1. Say, Can You Actually Learn It?

Frankly, that's the first thing people ask me when they hear that I teach happiness, right after they finish laughing and realize I'm being serious. In order to answer that question, we need to understand what happiness is.

Apparently, happiness is something we're born with. Believe it or not, according to research conducted over the last 50 years, ever since the beginning of happiness studies, 50% of our ability to feel happiness is genetic; that is – hereditary.[2]

Naturally, it depends on what has happened and still happens in our lives. But I was greatly surprised to find out that only 10% of our happiness depends on varying circumstances. That is, if we experience challenging and sad events or happy and pleasurable events, they will affect about 10% of our capacity to feel happy. Surprising, isn't it?

We can agree that 50% is quite a lot. That is, if half of our ability to feel happy is predetermined, and 10%

---

2. Lyubomirsky, Sonja, Kennon M. Sheldon, and David Schkade. "Pursuing happiness: The architecture of sustainable change." Review of general psychology 9.2 (2005): 111-131.

depends on our life's circumstances, is there anything that can be done?

Apparently, there is.

This is where I come in as a happiness coach. It would seem that the remaining 40% that determines our happiness has nothing to do with our life events or our parents. That depends solely on the way we perceive life and choose to behave.

As wise men have stipulated: "All is foreseen, but free will is given" (Avot, 3:15).

Everything is foreseen; this is the reality we live in, and we cannot actually control the events that occur in this reality. However, we have free will to choose how we interpret the events happening around us. Whether we live in heaven or in hell is up to our perception and the way we choose to see our lives.

So yes, we can learn happiness. We'll think together, throughout this book, about how to interpret our reality in a way that will make us happier, and enable us to optimize the 40% that is still available to us in our bank of happiness.

2. Happiness Takes on Many Forms

One of the first researchers to have studied happiness in modern times was Professor Daniel Kahneman, who was awarded a Nobel Prize for his prospect theory. In the 1990s, a little while before Kahneman received the award, he researched happiness and how we can increase its presence in our lives. The first problem that this very wise man had to tackle was: How can we define "happiness"?

Kahneman claimed that happiness was found in the "Experiencing Self," somewhat akin to mindfulness. Being in the here and now and enjoying the experience I'm currently experiencing is the secret to happiness according to Kahneman. But much to his surprise, a great number of researchers and research participants thought that happiness was found in the "Remembering Self." In other words, not in the experience itself, but in reminiscing and remembering the satisfaction derived from a past experience. Especially the way that the experience was perceived after it had occurred.[3] In other words, happiness is found in the way we interpret a certain event, rather than the feeling we have during the experience as it unfolds. This emphasizes the importance of our perception of reality, and not just reality itself. This is precisely what I teach with my *Seven Portals of Happiness* methodology.

---

3. Mendel Amir. "Forget About Happiness, Let's Talk About Preventing Agony" (interview with Professor Daniel Kahneman). Haaretz, October 2nd, 2018.

DEFINITIONS OF HAPPINESS

Throughout the years, scholars have been searching for the meaning of happiness. What they have found is that happiness has many definitions. The word "happiness" is used in the Old Testament. "And Leah said, 'Happy am I! For women have called me happy. So she called his name Asher.'" (Genesis 30:13) That is, happiness is linked to external validation. On the other hand, the words "happiness" and "luck" are interlinked in many European languages. In English, the word "hap" means a fortunate occasion; in German, the word *glück* means both happiness and luck. Happiness, thus, is perceived as something unexpected, a stroke of luck. In Buddhism, the transcendent goal in life is to reach a state of Nirvana, also referred to as a state of "idyllic happiness," and the path to achieving that coveted state is by disconnecting one's self from personal desires and completely giving in to reality as it is, acceptance and surrender.

In Ancient Greece, people believed that happiness is brought on by living a life full of meaning; reaching that would require maximizing one's potential. If an individual could live up to their potential in the best way possible – they were happy. However, Epicureans and Stoics vastly disagreed, the former claiming that a leisurely life is vital for happiness, while the latter maintaining that happiness is all about self-exploration.

3. The Hedonistic Treadmill, or Why Things Stop Making Us Happy

A couple of years ago, I stood in line at the supermarket deli. When my turn came, I asked the butcher for a large number of chicken filets. One man who was standing beside me. He pleasantly smiled and asked: "Are you having the grandchildren over for dinner?" I looked at him, appalled, and replied: "I don't have any grandchildren! Yet!"

Then, I decided it was time for a makeover.

I went on a short yet vigorous shopping spree. I bought a couple of lovely dresses from my favorite local designer, then booked an appointment at the hairdresser for a fresh hairdo. Next, I decided that all I was missing was a pair of gray boots that would perfectly complement the new dress I had bought. However, I couldn't find just the right pair, even though I tried many different stores. Do you know that feeling of when you really want something but can't find it? So that!

Frankly, I was quite upset. I said to myself, *Well, never mind. It's almost spring, anyways, maybe I'll find a pair of boots next winter...*

That's when I found myself at a mall I had never been to. I happened to wander into a brand-new shoe store. Right there, in the very middle of the "sale" section, the boots of my dreams awaited. They were the perfect color, the perfect height, and were on discount! I walked out with a bag full of boots and a heart full of happiness. It's a good thing I have ears because I smiled so widely that otherwise, my jaw would have dropped.

Does this story mean that this book is redundant? That all we actually need to achieve happiness is to find our ideal pair of boots? Well, no. Not at all. One of the main issues with happiness being derived from achieving certain goals or obtaining objects is that such happiness is temporary, fleeting, and, at times, leaves a bitter taste of disappointment. In happiness studies, this phenomenon is called the "Hedonic Treadmill." It's a metaphor for the surge of happiness we feel after a positive event, or the lack of happiness caused by a negative event. Such effects erode over time, as we are all likely to return to our personal happiness baseline. Achieving a goal could potentially bring me joy, but in and of itself, it won't increase my happiness in life. Because, as we've previously mentioned, sustainable happiness isn't a result; it's a journey, and in order to set off on that expedition, you need a map.

4. A Treasure(d) Map of Happiness

When our daughter Ofer was three years old, my beloved Odi and I considered having a fourth child. Ofer is our third, and when she was born, we felt that we had a "full house." We had a boy and two girls. They were all adorable, clever, and funny. And yet, the thought of having a fourth child appealed to us.

I started discussing the idea with my friends, who were older than me. Everyone I had spoken to about the matter had never said something like: "I regret having another child." However, people did say, over and over again, "we thought about having another child, and in fact, I regret that we didn't do it." It had nothing to do with how many children they had, or whether they were still married to their spouse. I decided that this wouldn't be something I'd regret later in life. And so, we were blessed with Noam.

Bronnie Ware,[4] an Australian palliative nurse, has conducted research about regret and concluded that people on their deathbeds had very similar regrets mostly about being disappointed for not having been true to themselves and having spent too much time working and not enough time with their family and friends. It served as a huge indicator for me as to where our happiness truly lies: Our happiness lies in our relationships with ourselves and others.

When a person looks back on their life before they pass away, they reflect on things that are genuinely important. Regret, therefore, stems from moments or events where we could have chosen differently, but ended up making a decision that did not result in our increased happiness. People on their deathbeds essentially regret not having lived the life that they desired. They regret living the life that was expected of them. They had spent too much time at work, and not enough time with their family. They weren't brave enough to fully express their feelings and they didn't spend enough time with their friends. As a result, they didn't allow themselves to be happy. Thus, by mapping the negative, we create the ideal map: a treasured map to happiness.

---

4. Ware, Bronnie. The top five regrets of the dying: A life transformed by the dearly departing. Hay House, Inc, 2012.

5. Our Happiness Lies Within Our Relationships

What makes us happier: winning the lottery or being in a car accident that leaves us with a permanent disability?

Apparently, being disabled enables us to retrieve our happiness levels from prior to the accident, whereas winning the lottery results in a somewhat decreased level of happiness.[5]

This isn't the only surprising finding about happiness. Studies show that while significant milestones in life do have an impact on our happiness, it is our day-to-day life that determines whether we are happy or not.

Harvard University has been researching happiness and health since 1938.[6] The research subjects were nineteen years old when the study began, and currently have almost reached their nineties. When the research started, the participants thought that experiencing professional success or financial gain would make them happy. They thought that their path of happiness would demand hard work and sacrifice. But it would seem that the central finding of this unique study was that neither money nor success evoked happiness; in fact, good relationships were the main source of happiness and health.

The Seven Portals model is almost an instructional guide that teaches us how to handle our relationships with ourselves and others, so we can reap all the happiness that lies within these relationships.

5. Brickman, Philip, Dan Coates, and Ronnie Janoff-Bulman. "Lottery winners and accident victims: Is happiness relative?" Journal of personality and social psychology 36.8 (1978): 917.

6. Vaillant, George E. "Triumphs of experience." Triumphs of Experience. Harvard University Press, 2012.

6. Having Choices is Happiness

Every morning, I find myself standing at a significant crossroads. Or perhaps, more accurately, every morning, I find myself lying at a significant crossroads on my bed. I open my eyes then shut them again, and check with myself what kind of day I am going to create for myself. Waking up every morning is the most meaningful part of my life so far, because at that very moment I can choose what the rest of my life will look like from that moment on.

I can wake up, and even before I have opened my eyes, reconnect with yesterday's anger, sense of a missed opportunity or loss, and different anxieties that can always resurface. However, I can always take another moment, indulge in that pleasant sensation between the pillow and sheets, relish in the softness of the mattress, and soak up the delightful numbness of my body still sleepily stretching in bed. Then, I can decide that this satisfying sensation will follow me throughout the day, even if reality throws challenging experiences my way. That is why this is the most important crossroads of my life. Every single morning.

Life can always confront us with agonizing events; this can be anything from losing a beloved relative and struggling financially to losing one's social status. It can be physical pain or a disease. Whatever it is, it's because pain is a part of the fabric of life. We cannot go through life without experiencing some measure of pain. But we can always choose how to handle that pain. When pain does arrive, it's important that we recognize it and acknowledge it. That being said, we can choose whether to become addicted to pain or experience it and then let it go. No type of pain, as severe as it may be, exists ceaselessly and hurts us each and every moment. Once the pain is alleviated, we can choose whether we should enjoy that pain-free moment or cling to the pain and embrace it.

7. Happiness is an Expedition

Seven Portals is a method that utilizes existing knowledge about the factors of happiness and the ways it can be attained, and transforms this knowledge into practical tools. These tools can allow each and every one of us to enjoy a better life, because the Seven Portals is a way of life.

Happiness isn't a clear goal that can be conquered; it isn't something that we can acquire. We can't just get our happily ever after; happiness isn't a diploma that can be hung on a wall. Happiness is an essence; it's a state of consciousness that we choose to live within. Happiness is a perspective on reality. Happiness is derived from an ensemble of choices, behaviors, and patterns that we select at any given moment.

There are seven states of awareness that once we practice them, they can assist us in creating a better and happier life, even if our objective reality remains exactly the same. These states of awareness are the Seven Portals, each of which will allow you to enter the "City of Happiness" – the very state in which we want to exist. Each of these portals improves our relationship with ourselves and with others. These portals are states of awareness that shape the way we conduct ourselves throughout life. The portals are: Giving, Acceptance, Gratitude, Compassion, Joy, Forgiveness, and Love. Each of these states is a substantial portal allowing you to enter a state of daily happiness.

It's important that we remember that happiness isn't a singular act. Every day, every moment is never the ending point of the process; it is a milestone. Happiness is an essence, which means that we need to behave and carry ourselves in a certain way in order to live in a conscious state of happiness. Happiness is the path I choose to take, and at any given moment, I can use the Seven Portals in order to choose to be happy under certain circumstances.

I'm often asked what is the first step we can and should take in order to be happy. Happiness frequently begins with a clear desire: knowing what I want. We'll further discuss this matter in the next chapter.

What the Heck

Do I Want?

What the Heck Do I Want?

8. She Sat in Front of Me and Her Tears Rolled Silently

She didn't whimper, nor whine; only the tears rolling down her cheeks revealed her emotional storm. A couple of minutes later, she said in a trembling voice: "But why? Why aren't I satisfied? Why am I constantly sad? I have everything. So, what the heck do I want?"

I looked into her teary eyes and wondered how long she had been feeling that way. How many years has she been living someone else's life, unable to understand why she can't feel happy even though she "has everything?"

When we're born, our desires are clear-cut.

If a baby is hungry, wet, or wants some affection, it expresses that need in a very simple way: it cries. When a baby has an unfulfilled desire, it can sway the people around it to meet that need. As we grow up, life, our parents, or society teach us that our desires can't always be fulfilled. Then, we start accumulating:

Disappointments: each time our desire isn't fulfilled.

Criticism: when we express our desire but it doesn't align with our environment's values or agenda.

We then feel **ashamed** of our desires and wants.

And so, bit by bit, through socialization and internalization, we learn to stop listening to our desires. We drown out the connection that we have with our inner voice. We conceal and ignore our dreams and wants, and instead, we adopt desires that we perceive as worthier, better, and more significant. And when that inner voice of ours tries to address us, we silence it with **shame**, **disregard,** and **belittlement of** our genuine desires.

This act of suppression and self-silencing disconnects us from our real desires and our inner voice, and is in fact the source of a lot of our pain and sadness. Realizing what the heck we want isn't some game; it's a serious challenge that brings us closer to who we are and enables us to define our goals and values in life. It's our compass on the path of happiness.

9. Three Wishes

Let us imagine that I find an old lamp, pick it up, and rub it. Let's also imagine that a genie emerges from it – the genie of the lamp. The genie tells me that he can grant me three wishes.

Well, first, I'd wish to have enough money to buy anything I want. But then, I'd find myself in a pickle; I'd have two more wishes that cannot be attainable objects – like an iPhone or a mansion – because I've covered those with my first wish. The moment money isn't an issue and I can have anything that money can buy, what more would I want?

In my opinion, this is exactly where the true meaning of life begins. What do I want that cannot be bought?

Where can I find my magic W.A.N.D?

W.A.N.D is a new concept I had thought of and is in fact somewhat magical. It stands for Wants and Desires. As I've learned from one of my beloved teachers: Wants and desires are markers along our inner journey to finding the meaning of life. When we listen to our wants and desires, we can perform our day-to-day tasks with passion.

But finding "what I want" is no simple task. Years of education and reprimand have deeply instilled in us the understanding that what I want is unimportant, impossible, far-fetched, irrational, etc.

I believe that every change for the better starts with a very basic understanding of what on earth I do want. Otherwise, I might find myself chasing consumer goods, when all I really want is to fill that pit in my stomach. Because what I truly want is by now so meek and pale it's been rendered into a lump of dissatisfaction; and I fail to understand why I feel so miserable, even though I've bought the latest iPhone on the market.

10. Why is It So Hard for Me to Figure Out What I Want?

As adults, we become more distant from ourselves. We don't always have a clear understanding of what we want, and when we do, we're unsure of why we have those specific desires. As children, we know how to express our desires in an obvious way. "I wanna" is commonly used by children. Then their parents often reply, "You mean 'I want.'" While parents are clearly trying to educate their children on how to properly express themselves, they're also actually saying: "Your desires aren't as important as your words." If my wants and wishes are less significant to my parents, who are my role models in life, what does that say about the significance of my desires?

It means that my desire isn't important enough to be taken seriously, or valid enough to be negotiated. It means that I'm being expected, at a young age, to realize that my wants and wishes, which are my milestones through life, aren't important to my parents who are the most important people in my life. This insight pushes children to suppress their inner desires, and start paying attention to their surroundings instead of listening to themselves.

The parents, who set the disconnection process into motion, intend no harm. Based on their life experiences, wishes don't come true, and it's best if their child internalizes that realization because otherwise, they'll find themselves experiencing disappointment. You could say that it's a subconscious parenting defense mechanism.

But there is one crucial distinction. Knowing what I want doesn't necessarily guarantee that I'll get it; however, it does create inner serenity that comes from self-awareness. It would be more efficient teaching children to express their wishes and negotiate with their surroundings, as they try to reconcile what is possible within the framework of these desires instead of silencing those desires in order to protect them from disappointments.

11. So, the Big Question is: Where is My Inner Voice?

I meet people in my clinic who have lost their ability to recognize what they desire. The culture we live in intensifies this phenomenon where we disconnect from our true desire. For instance, we find this phenomenon in the world of advertising. This form of disconnection increases the financial profit of various manufacturers that sell us "desire substitutes." After years of suppressing our true desires, corporations and manufacturers of different commodities advertise their products as the so-called answer to our desires. Furthermore, since we've lost contact with our true desires, we buy these replacements in order to fill the void caused by this loss to begin with. That is the foundation of a consumerism-based economy.

Every commercial appeals to the gaping pit within us caused by our inability to identify our true desires. These commercials subconsciously tell us: "Here is your desire, and we have a product that can fulfill this desire." Thus, they prevent us from silently reconnecting with our inner voice, our true desire, and what we authentically want.

For years, I've been giving my patients at the clinic a simple exercise: pause several times every day at regular intervals and ask yourself "What do I want right now?" Then, wait a couple of minutes to find the answer. It sounds simple and easy, but since we're accustomed to silencing our desires, hearing that inner voice again might take some time. When it does happen, we need to nurture and empower that voice like a newborn. The stronger it grows, the more we should listen to it because that is the true voice of our hearts.

12. Decisions are No Simple Matter

When I speak to people in my clinic, they often bring up their difficulty in making decisions. This difficulty frustrates and even hurts them. So, what is it that prevents us from making decisions?

Usually, our inability to make a decision stems from our fear of the consequences. What if I make the wrong choice? What if I'm making a mistake?

But, why do we think that we might make a mistake? After all, making a decision means that I have the power to choose. So, I can consider all options and choose what I want. Can't I?

In my opinion, this is where the true issue lies: our difficulty in realizing what we actually want.

Sometimes, our life seems like one long boot camp training session of "let us hide our real desires so that one day I won't know what the heck I want either."

Let's start with our education. Parents and educational figures have been telling children for years that their wants and wishes are irrelevant. What matters is what the system, their families, and society require. Thus, children grow up believing that their desire is unimportant. Slowly, their inner voice dies out; at first, it shouts to them, next it speaks, and then it only whispers. "I want" is being silenced because it's either impossible right now, isn't convenient, or it's not how things are done, etc.

One of the most important things I teach in my clinic is the use of the magic W.A.N.D – our wants and desires – because they represent our primal and genuine connection to ourselves.

13. Using Our GPS (Typing in the Right Destination)

I'm the master of getting lost. When I was in the fifth grade, I had to go to my scout's activity on my own because all my friends couldn't make it that day. I had walked there dozens of times before with my friends, but this time, I was alone. After half an hour of wandering around, I realized I had no idea where I was. To make matters worse, I didn't know the way back home. After another half hour, I managed to recognize a familiar street, made one right turn, and made it home as I always did: two-and-a-half hours later. Yet this time, I hadn't been to my activity. I was happy, however, that I managed to return home because for a minute there, I was unsure I would.

Now, I already know that if I think I should take a right, it probably means I should take a left in order to reach my destination. In the past, navigating somewhere required a detailed map and plenty of U-turns. But there's one invention that saved my life, and that's the GPS. Today, I get into my car, type in the destination I need to reach, and from that moment on, there's someone who guides me, telling me where to turn, and all n I need to do is follow its directions.

Our journey in life is just like any other. When we start driving our car, it's usually because we have a certain goal – a destination we want to reach. If we want to reach a certain city but type in another we won't make it to our desired destination. As long as I keep typing in that other city, it doesn't matter where my starting point is; the GPS will never take me to my required goal. But, what does that have to do with what I want? Our desires are our journey's destinations. However, a variety of different factors prevent us from pinpointing that specific destination because our desire remains uncertain.

Often, due to life's circumstances and the way we were raised, our inner voice is drowned out to the point where sometimes it's completely silenced because it stops believing that we care about it. The result is that we aim to accomplish desires that are allegedly ours but in fact are not. They're what we think we need to desire and what we assume that we should desire. However, we find ourselves in a situation where we have allegedly acquired what we wanted, and yet remain unhappy, dissatisfied, and more generally unable to understand what's wrong with us and why we can't just be satisfied.

14. Rebuilding Our Inner Voice's Trust in Ourselves

The first part of our expedition towards happiness is reconnecting to that inner voice so that we can become attentive towards our desires. One of the main challenges to rebuilding our inner voice's trust in us is our inability to answer a desire when it appears from within. It's important to note that we shouldn't immediately adhere to it. Instead, we should acknowledge that we heard that desire and that it's been noted. Even if we cannot instantly fulfill that desire, it's being taken care of.

For instance, our inner voice says: I want to be in Thailand right now!

Okay, I realize that you want to be in Thailand, but there's a pandemic and no one can travel. Perhaps we could go to the beach, or kick back on my porch and enjoy a tropical shake until I can in fact reach Thailand. In other words, I'm acknowledging my desire, and then I'm **negotiating** with my inner voice regarding what can be satisfied now and what can be addressed later on. And so, gradually, my inner voice will resume talking to me, and I'll discover my real desire.

15. Recognizing the Essence and Negotiating

People often struggle to listen to their inner voice that is telling them what they truly want because they think that if they can hear what they want they'll need to immediately answer that desire. And yet, they frequently find themselves unsure as to how they can fulfill that desire and meet their needs.

The best way is to clarify the essence at the heart of that desire. Let us go back to the Thailand example. That desire can embody several desires: Perhaps it's an expression of my desire for time off and having some peace of mind. Perhaps it's a desire to have fun, or maybe it's a desire to spend alone time with someone close without being interrupted by others: just you and that person at a remote location.

Each of these examples represents a different desire.

If flying to Thailand is currently impossible, perhaps identifying the essence of the desire will allow us to address that essence and fulfill that specific desire. If I yearn for a break, perhaps taking a long weekend off or even asking the kids' grandparents to babysit for a couple of days and switching off my phone could fulfill that desire.

If I crave having fun or having a good time, perhaps exchanging homes with someone from a different city could do the trick. Once we recognize the core desire, we can negotiate with our inner voice and target the essence.

Sometimes, I'm afraid of listening to myself because I'm worried that I'll have to completely turn my life upside down in order to satisfy that inner voice. It usually manifests with regard to meaningful relationships that seemingly no longer make me happy, or workplaces. That is, it could be anything that on the one hand drives me off and on the other is inevitable. In those cases, I don't listen to my inner voice because I feel stuck and out of options. Ignoring our inner voice in such cases over and over again may lead to more severe problems that eventually, reluctantly force us to look our issues straight in the eye.

16. When We Don't Want, We Don't Get Hurt?

Sometimes, people tell me: "I don't want to want; wanting leads to pain and disappointment. When we don't want, we don't get hurt."

So, let's set things straight. It isn't the wish or desire that leads to pain; it's the doubt and concern that my desire won't come true that actually hurts us.

When I want and I don't let fear seep into my desire, when I yearn from a place of confidence, the desire becomes sheer pleasure and it's delightful. Let us take for example something simple like ice cream. If I really want some ice cream, then I probably know exactly what flavors I want and the level of the desired crunchiness of the ice cream cone. I can practically feel the sweet cream melt in my mouth. Ice cream is easily attainable. When I crave ice cream, I can easily savor the very act of desire. However...

When I crave ice cream and tell myself: "But it's high in sugar," or "dairy isn't healthy, it's cruel and it's f-a-t-t-e-n-i-n-g!" The desire becomes painful because I doubt or fear that this simple desire cannot come true.

Putting the ice cream aside, this is an important insight, because our desire can be for success, love, riches, and belonging. The desire itself isn't flawed. Our desires are perfect just the way they are. But the very minute we doubt them or their ability to come true, we turn that desire into pain.

17. How My Real Desire is Connected to the Universe's Grand Design

About a year ago, Dave and Myra paid us a visit from distant Seattle. Dave told our children how I boarded his fishing boat in Alaska and was the first woman who had joined his crew. He was already a seasoned skipper at that time.

"She just kept nagging me until I realized I didn't have

a choice," Dave told Ofer and Noam, who listened to his story with amazement. They both laughed: "Yep, that's our mom!"

"Hang on," I cut him off, "what do you mean? I didn't nag you or force you to take me on that fishing trip. You needed a cook, I approached you without any cooking experience, and you simply decided to accept me. That's precisely what happened if I'm not mistaken."

All three looked at me and burst out laughing.

So, I started to ponder as I often do when I realize there's a gap between the way I perceive reality and how others perceive it.

I arrived in Alaska totally unannounced, with one thought in mind: to finish having the "Where is this going" talk with Odi. We'd started discussing that question three months earlier, but then, poof, Odi took off to Alaska to fish on a fishing boat in the Bering Sea on that same fishing boat where Dave was the skipper.

I'll tell the story of how I simply showed up unannounced in the Middle of Nowhere Alaska later on in this book. But for now, for the purpose of this story, I want to discuss our ability to focus on a certain idea or a certain thought, and how we can build our reality around it.

When I set off and headed to Alaska, into the unknown on that summer more than thirty years ago, I knew for certain that I was going away for a long time. I made sure to ask my cousin to dog-sit. I told my mother that she couldn't worry because I didn't know when I'd come back or if I could stay in touch. I knew I was going to board that fishing boat, no matter what.

I didn't know there would only be men on the boat,

or that if we combined their jail terms together, we'd get two or three life sentences (each and every one of them was a charmer, by the way). I had no idea that the boat sets sail and doesn't return until it's full of fish, even if this meant being at sea for a whole month even during a storm when the waves towered 15 feet or more. I did know two things: I had a conversation to finish, and I wanted to be on that boat!

I call it the ability to focus on a specific concept or a certain idea and build your reality around it. When we're connected to our desires, we don't settle for something because that's just the way things are. This by no means implies that you should have a full-blown tantrum, throw yourself on the floor, and scream out "I want it!" until someone finally gives in and satisfies you. Instead, I am referring to being persistent about finding that window after a door has been slammed in your face.

When I want something, and it doesn't happen the way I had imagined it, I don't give up on the final outcome. I listen attentively to the universe and keep checking for a window to crack open.

I don't believe in going head-to-head with a brick wall. I believe in marking a target, knowing what I want to feel and what I find important, and knowing the essence of what I hope to attain. Then I head towards that target while paying attention to the path. As my father-in-law would put it: "The path is wiser than those who walk it."

When I know what I want, even if a door is shut, our Happiness GPS recalculates our route and continues to lead us on our expedition of happiness. So, whether I receive what I wanted or not, I make sure to fine-tune myself and find another way. When the destination is known, and our desire is well-defined, the universe leads the way for us.

'How Does Speakin 'Universish

Increase Happiness?

How Does Speaking 'Universish' Increase Happiness?

18. Why Should You Learn to Speak Universish?

I believe that according to the laws of the universe, we affect and make choices out of the infinite potential life paths that are available to us. Unfortunately, most of us make these choices subconsciously for two reasons. The first reason is because we grow up believing that we don't really have the power to influence our reality; some of us even believe that we're victims of our lives' circumstances. The second reason is due to the education and culture that we've discussed in the previous chapter. We disconnect from our inner voice and stop recognizing our true desires.

The deeper I dive into the matter, the more I realize that what changes things for me is my awareness of what I actually want. Often, the environment, external factors, and other things that are completely unrelated to my desires affect what I want. I make choices that allegedly enable me to achieve what I desire, but the result doesn't make me happy or even pleased.

Therefore, if I can't pinpoint my desire for myself, my feelings and actions will attract results, out of the infinite potential options that will disappoint me, and reinforce the sense that I'm a victim of life's circumstances, and don't really have any control.

However, the truth is to the contrary.

It's a little like stepping into an extremely smart car that I can't drive, and instead of learning how to operate it, I take the car on a test drive. I'll probably end up thinking that the car isn't great, and I won't stop to think that perhaps it was me who couldn't figure out how to drive it.

19. How We Didn't Visit Thailand and a Thank You Goes to the Universe

In December 2004, Odi and I decided to visit Thailand with our four children. "This time," I said to Odi, "we're going to Phuket."

"Come on..." my beloved husband replied, "Phuket is swarming with tourists – it isn't Thailand at all."

"I don't care," I insisted. "We've already been to Thailand twice and we still haven't visited Phuket. Besides, everyone goes to Phuket, so it must be awesome and I want to be there too!"

"Okay," my dear husband was appeased, "whatever you say. If you want Phuket – we'll visit Phuket."

For several weeks prior to our planned trip, I sat in front of my laptop and tried to book our dream vacation in Phuket. I looked for family-friendly hotels and contacted them. Some told me that they were booked solid, and the others didn't give me an answer at all. I tried finding a family car, but there were none to be found. In short, nothing worked right. About two weeks before our flight, when I realized I couldn't make it work, I said to Odi: "Listen, I don't know what's up with our trip to Phuket; nothing's working out for me!"

"You know what," my beloved partner replied, "let's go to Costa Rica."

I sat down in front of my computer, and within days I managed to book a wonderful vacation for us in Costa Rica. We traveled there and had a great time. Because we were in the Americas, we decided to visit friends in Los Angeles and stay with them for the last couple of days of our vacation. As we were sitting on their sofa, we saw the tsunami in Phuket on TV.

I looked up and whispered, "I get it. You didn't have to hurt so many people, but I promise to listen from now on."

That event was a turning point for me, because for the first time, I had a crystal-clear realization that the universe was talking to us and guiding us. If we only listen, fine-tune our attention, and make decisions accordingly, we'll find ourselves in the right place at the right time instead of being in the wrong place at the wrong time.

This was the first time I took a close look at the universe's "no." If you've ever taken care of children, then you know that "no" is a magic word. When we want to protect our little ones, especially from themselves, we tend to say "no." While it's true that some educational theories object to using the word "no" as an instructional tool (some even go as far as banning the word "no" completely), as a mother of four who has previously owned a daycare, I know that "no" is powerful and has the potential of saving lives.

No doubt that traditional educational approaches have abused the word "no," leading us to having an aversion to it. We resist the "no" and sometimes, even ignore it. Furthermore, we overuse the word "no" with ourselves because we're motivated by fear that prevents us from doing things that might be beneficial. But when we converse with the universe, "no" is a crucial word, and it's important that we listen to it and let it guide us towards the best course of action.

20. "No!" is the Universe's Way of Telling Us: Hang On, Stop, Listen Here

When I encounter a "no" I stop to look around. I then check my own magic W.A.N.D (Wants and Desires). This means that I need to discern whether this "no" refers to something that I actually want or maybe I need to fine-tune my desire.

Then, I define more clearly what I truly want, and take the next step according to that realization.

Throughout that process, I'm guided by my faith in the universe's wisdom. The universe doesn't want to toy with me or hurt me. The universe aspires for every seed to flourish and reach its full potential, be it a rose, a goldfish, or myself. The universe is here to help me fully blossom.

And what does all that have to do with "gratuitous love?"

The more I believe that the universe is working in my favor, the easier it is for me to root for other people and offer my love and advice just for the sake of giving. Therefore, the more fluent I become in Universish, the more happiness I experience in my life.

21. Just a Sec. So, by 'Universish' – You Mean Karma?

When people ask me whether Universish is actually Karma, it reminds me of Sogyal Rinpoche's story in his book *The Tibetan Book of Living and Dying* (published in 1992).

The book tells the story of a man who sat on a rock by the riverbank and saw someone drowning.

He said to himself: "I don't need to do a thing, because drowning is probably his karma."

To which Rinpoche replies with a question: How do you know that your karma isn't saving him?

Sometimes, we tend to think that spirituality negates our need to take action in the material world. If the universe said "no," maybe from now on, I should sit on the sofa and do nothing. But I don't think that's true. I think that sincere spirituality is expressed by taking action in the material world driven by a true connection to our inner spirit. Spirituality is not powered by the belief in the triumph of spirit over matter, because happiness isn't a power struggle between those two; it's a fruitful collaboration.

22. Speaking 'Universish' – Eases the Pain

"So I saw that there is nothing better for a person than to enjoy their work, because that is their lot." (Ecclesiastes 3:22)

Earlier this week, someone asked me at the clinic whether I'm talking about compliance. I was very surprised by her question because compliance is so far from what I'm talking about.

So no, I'm absolutely not talking about compliance. I'm talking about attentiveness for the purpose of finding joy and finding the good that lies in everything that happens to us. There's a plot line in the movie *Fried Green Tomatoes* about a boy who loses one of his arms in a train accident. Idgie, the movie's hero, shows him a three-legged puppy that races with the other dogs and beats them all. She explains that he can choose to feel miserable and pity himself, or he can understand that his path in life entails having only one arm and yet he can still be the most amazing of the bunch.

We all know people whose disability, rough life, and trials could have made them give up, call it a day, and be done. But it's the way they handled the difficulty that led to great achievements. Think about Stephen Hawking, who developed spectacular theories while sitting in a wheelchair and communicating through a computer and voice synthesizer activated with a single finger.

So, I'm not referring to compliance in the sense of compromise, but rather to being attentive in the sense of paying attention and realizing that although pain is a part of life, suffering is a choice. We all get an occasional "no" from the universe. Some "no's" hurt more than others, but when we comprehend that this rejection is a form of guidance and we choose to follow it, we can live our lives better.

23. Small Gifts from the Universe

Around Thanksgiving, Odi and I spent a couple of days in Corfu. It's a pleasant and pastoral island, located near the Greek shore that personally thrills me very much because that's where the stories from Gerald Durrell's *My Family and Other Animals* take place.

One morning, we decided to go on a road trip, drove to the other side of the island, and visited an exceptionally gorgeous vantage point. On the way back, Odi decided to take a different turn.

It's pretty easy letting the road lead us, especially when we're equipped with a GPS system (although we used to find our destinations way before GPS was accessible).

And so, we took a turn into a narrow and winding path. At the end, we saw a sign that read "Beach with Private Energy." Could we really have resisted such a sign?

We parked our car at the end of the road facing a rocky and somewhat cliffy shoreline. Then we continued on foot down the rocks.

Behind a large pile of rocks, a magnificent sight appeared. There were two beach chairs on the tiniest piece of land, just standing there and waiting for us in the middle of nowhere. Of course, we decided to join them and had a wonderful time enjoying our own private beach. That's what happens when you speak

Universish and are willing to accept all the wonderful gifts the universe sends your way.

24. When the Universe Knows Better

When my Noam was in the ninth grade, he decided that he really wanted to move to a boarding school. He found a unique one that housed talented kids from all over the country who chose to be together through high school. He was certain that it was the right place for him to spend the last three years of his secondary education.

He passed all their tests and assessments, and there were quite a few. Then, right before the very end when we knew he was practically in, they rejected him. He was heartbroken. I tried to console him and said: "Listen to me, we still don't know why, but it probably isn't the right place for you."

"Ugh, you and your universe," he grumbled. He wrote the school an appeal letter. The first words were: "I don't know how to tell you this, but you've made a huge mistake."

They replied saying that he was right, but that they no longer had a spot for him. He then stayed for another year at the local high school.

During that year in high school, he met a bunch of wonderful guys who became his life-long friends. One day he came back home and said: "Mom, I know why I wasn't accepted to that boarding school; I want to enroll in an international boarding school. There are many and they are spread throughout the world and located in fascinating places like Scotland, Armenia, or India. They visited our school today and told us about it."

He went through all the tests and assessments, and each time he finished one stage, he had to pass another. Then, after he passed them all and he was practically in, he received yet another rejection. Disappointment was in the air; we could taste the bitter sting of failure. Then someone told him about a different international boarding school that was closer to home. He casually sent his application to that boarding school. Again, one after another, an interview followed by another assessment, and then he was told he'd been waitlisted.

A couple of weeks later, they contacted him and offered an online interview with the boarding school principal. The interview was supposed to take place during his school day, and I couldn't pick him up on time. He therefore told them that he couldn't complete the interview. However, much to our surprise, we found out there was a parent's day that day and his school was sending all the kids home at noon. In other words, he was able to be home for the interview. Indeed, he did have that interview with the boarding school principal, who we found later on never interviews applicants. He was then accepted.

He started studying in September 2019. COVID broke out in March 2020. As a mother, I was so pleased that with all the madness going on, my son was nearby rather than stuck at some faraway boarding school in Armenia or Japan. Other than that, he had two wonderful years – the best we could have asked for. He studied with friends from all over the world and had unique experiences that made him extremely happy.

"The "Seven Portals of Happiness

Model

Welcome to the Portal

of Giving

Welcome to the Portal of Giving

25. THE PORTAL OF GIVING:
The Foundation of Every Relationship

Giving makes us happy because it allows us to feel that we are competent and that we make our own choices. These are two impactful feelings when it comes to our happiness levels. Being competent is the opposite of feeling helpless. Helplessness kills happiness; being competent, even if you find yourself in a difficult or painful situation, allows us to feel that we have the power to make a difference or a change, which contributes greatly to our sense of happiness.

The Opposite of Giving: The opposite of giving isn't receiving – it's appeasing. When we give in order to please others, we feel obligated to give, or compelled to give, it enhances our feelings of helplessness, preventing us from feeling happy. Thus we're "pushed out" of happiness.

Course of Action: Giving reinforces your sense of capability, competence, and control. However, if the act of giving is done in order to please or appease others and is driven by an obligation to maintain their love for me or to prevent them from abandoning me, then the giving is no longer empowering. It becomes appeasing, which in turn intensifies a sense of helplessness and reluctance. Therefore, it's important that we remain aware of our giving practices and make sure that they are motivated by a desire to give rather than a feeling of powerlessness of "I must give." Let's say I have to tend to my baby but in fact, I feel like going to the beach. If I tell myself "But it's my baby, whom I love very much, and I choose to take care of her," it changes things. It brings you closer to happiness than if you'd say something like, "Well, I don't have a choice. I have a baby and I need to take care of her."

26. Giving is Pleasurable

Many years ago, when my Ofer was still very little, we went on a family trip. It entailed many hours of driving; we were two parents with four children crammed into one car.

On one of our stops at some gas station, Ofer came with me to the bathroom. Of course, we had to walk through aisles of candy, snacks, and other temptations.

When we finished doing our business, I approached the register to pay for the gas. Ofer held up a bag of lollipops: "Can I have it? Please, Mommy? Can I?"

"Okay," I agreed. "Take the bag and go back to the car. I'll pay for it." When I returned to the car a couple of minutes later, I saw there was only one lollipop left in the bag. Apparently, she had shared all the lollipops with her brothers, sister, and Odi, and even shared the lollipops with two girls sitting in the car next to us. "Here, Mommy, this one's yours," she said happily.

"But Ofer, sweetie, what about you? You didn't get a lollipop!"

"It's okay, mommy. I got to hand them out – sharing is caring," she replied smilingly.

27. Giving or Appeasing

I enjoy giving. I reached this insight a couple of years ago. My true essence – the spark that keeps me going – is giving. When I give, I'm happy. Throughout my life, somewhere between the age of thirty and fifty, I had to learn to put a limit on my giving just so I could refine it for myself and for those on the receiving end. I suppose the best way to describe it is by picturing a person who says she's addicted to chocolate. She tells herself that she mustn't have any chocolate at all, but she struggles to curb her desire. The reason for this challenge is that she shouldn't forbid herself from eating, but rather should listen to herself when she craves chocolate. Only if she truly listens to her desire can she moderate herself and clarify the amount of chocolate that she truly desires every time. The same goes for me with giving. Today, I'm in the most balanced place I have ever been.

The issue with being addicted to giving is that we can very easily shift from pure giving to a feeling of fear that if we don't give, people might stop loving us. In this case, we lose the advantages of giving and fall into pleasing. When I give to please, instead of feeling satisfied and happy with giving I become frustrated or even angry.

I feel that I'm being compelled to give, even if it's me who's forcing myself to give.

Similar to the chocolate bar scenario, listening inwardly does the trick. Let's say I got a stomachache after scarfing down a whole chocolate bar without listening to my inner voice, when I only wanted just a little chocolate; yet because I was afraid that I wouldn't let myself eat any more if I wanted some later, I ate the whole thing. The same goes for giving. We want to give, but we need to be attentive to the reason behind it. Otherwise, we'll spiral into pleasing and feeling bad again (or nauseous).

28. It's Not Us, It's Evolution

Let's take a minute to talk about humanity as a whole. As you know, during COVID we realized, more than ever, how much we are all connected and depend on one another. We understood the extent to which someone's actions in China can affect someone living in Italy. I'm not only referring to the fact that this interconnectivity allows Italian women to buy cheaper clothes at Zara. I am referring to the sense that we are interdependent.

In his book *Sapiens: A Brief History of Humankind* (published in 2013), Yuval Noah Harari demonstrates that the single factor that has contributed to the rise of humankind as the ruling species on planet Earth is human beings' social skills. He refers to our ability to communicate and exchange information about things that don't exist yet, to invent and think different thoughts, and to communicate these thoughts to others. But the most important factor is our ability to collaborate.

The fact that I had originally typed these words in Hebrew while using a keyboard that was manufactured in China, and that these words will be read in English and printed via American technology is in itself proof of the grand marvel that is humankind's collaboration.

Most of us know that our development and advancement progress according to the rules of evolution. This means that a change that occurs due to adaptation to the existing environment will become permanent and evolve into the next phase of our development. This is true for biology, but it is also true for our social and spiritual development.

Since collaborations are the true power of humankind, evolution has functioned as a driving force. Similarly, findings from a study conducted in 2012 show that children under the age of two are inclined to share, which in turn makes them happy. Children under the age of two find giving more enjoyable than receiving; in fact, they're even happier when they give something of their own than when they give some random object. Furthermore, a study performed in 2013 discovered that giving activates pleasure centers in the brain.In other words, there's a neurological connection between giving and happiness.

A majority of us were raised to believe that there's never enough and that this is a dog-eat-dog world, but these studies prove the contrary!

We're neurologically wired to give.

From a very young age, before we could absorb capitalism's falsities, giving something of our own invoked a genuine sense of pleasure and happiness.

29. The Universe is All About Giving

The most important thing about giving, and perhaps which makes us happiest, is giving to fulfill a true need the receiver has. Their reaction often shows us just how accurate our giving was. And yet, sometimes, the receiver doesn't show whether our giving was accurate to their needs, so I re-examine what I gave, and the way I gave it. Then, I can decide whether I was right and precise, and the receiver will also realize it in due time, or I misunderstood the situation and I need to rectify it.

The greatest insight from all of this is... drumroll...that this is how the universe works!

The universe is all about giving, and its sole desire is to fine-tune its giving in order to ensure that it is the right thing for us at the right time.

If we fail to refine the vibe of what we desire, or if we're unclear on our desires, because we might be distracted by all the wonderful things other people have and our desires pale in comparison, and are perhaps obscure or unclear – then we might receive things that are imprecise.

Alternatively, we might think that what we received was inaccurate, but we eventually realize that it was just the right thing for us and our path. In other words, the giver knows better than the receiver what might answer the latter's needs.

That's the way the universe works. The universe provides us with accurate answers, but we don't always know how to receive them. What do you think: Is the universe generous and accurate when it gives?

Do you remember a time when the universe gave you

something that seemed to be wrong but turned out to be just right?

30. Giving is a Simple Everyday Practice

Sometimes, we think giving is complex and difficult and that it requires a lot of effort and attention. But giving also lies in a plethora of small and routine moments that build up throughout the day, week, month, and lifetime. For example:

One day, I woke up very early. Rotem, my eldest son, planned to leave for his friends' wedding up north. This occurred during COVID, a time that forced us to find unique and creative solutions for social events such as small home weddings and other celebrations which despite their limited size, were actually rife with joy. Our need for social meetings, which had no outlet during the lockdowns, was building up inside us and was generating great joy when given such an outlet.

Before he left the house, he asked me to help him wrap the unique gift he got Tammy and Thomas for their special day. Indeed, I helped him wrap the present, and we did a great job. We were both elated thanks to that small and simple act we did together. I felt that I was a really good mother, just because of a simple act of giving to my eldest son.

Since I had already woken up, I decided to leave earlier for my meeting downtown. People were still reluctant to leave their homes, so the roads weren't as busy as usual. I arrived at the meeting location half an hour early. I decided to have a nice cup of coffee at a lovely café.

When I sat down, I noticed a mother and her little girl trying to cross a bike path but to no avail.

The little girl was so sweet, and she looked at her surroundings with great interest.

I addressed her mother and said: "She's the cutest, and she looks just like you!"

The mother's face lit up: She grinned from ear to ear, bashfully thanked me, crossed the boulevard, and sat on the bench in front of me. She had obviously enjoyed the small "gift" I had given her when I complimented her daughter. And me?

Well, my heart swelled with joy knowing that I made her happy. That was the second time I had given to someone that day. I felt uplifted for the rest of the day.

On my way back home, I stopped at a supermarket and pushed the shopping cart along the aisles. Suddenly, I saw a very old and quite short lady who was unsuccessfully trying to reach a product on one of the higher shelves. She looked around helplessly. As a reminder, I should mention this was at the height of the pandemic and everyone was practicing social distancing. As a result, she couldn't grab anyone's attention and seemed pretty lost.

So I said to her: "Excuse me, ma'am, could you take a step back?" I reached out to the highest shelf and took the product she wanted. She replied, "That one too, please," then pointed at another product. I grabbed that one as well. I placed both of the products on a lower shelf, then stepped back to make sure she'd feel safe enough to take the products. Remember that time? When we all still thought COVID was some lethal, highly-contagious plague? She approached the shelf, took the products, and said: "Thank you so much! Happy holidays."

I resumed shopping, and my heart sang like a bird that had been freed from its cage.

That's exactly the way it works: A small act of giving such as a compliment, or lending a hand to our loved ones or complete strangers can bring happiness into a mundane day, transforming it into a miraculous day.

31. Giving is Actually Good for Your Health

"A generous person will prosper; whoever refreshes others will be refreshed" (Proverbs 11:25).

One of the most interesting things about giving, beyond the fact that it simply makes us happy, is that giving improves our health. That's right, it's as simple as that.

Allow me to wear my doctor hat for a moment: As early as the 1980s, researchers started collecting data that showed that people who give enjoy health advantages compared to those who are self-centered and take care mostly of themselves.

True, it seems somewhat strange and odd to our Western-capitalistic perspective. How could caring for others make me feel better? But this is exactly what studies show.

For instance, in a study from 2006, researchers discovered that people who have a tendency to provide social support to others have lower blood pressure, higher self-esteem, and are less likely to suffer from stress or depression. Their general health was shown to be better than those who do not provide support to others.

The researchers successfully separated between the act of giving social support and receiving support and proved that engaging in giving improved physical and mental health indicators.

Another study published in 2013 found that people who gave aid to others during that year were less likely to die of stress-induced conditions compared to those who didn't. It might sound absurd, but giving can actually save lives.

That is to say, aside from the general happiness that giving brings us, it also creates neurological links that have a positive impact on our general health in several aspects.

32. Giving Reduces Sadness

Earlier today, I received an email from a cosmetics company about today being "International Siblings Day." To celebrate, they were offering some sort of discount on their soap. That email made me feel deeply sad, and miss my deceased brothers terribly. When I'm sad, I allow myself to feel that sadness, but I make sure not to immerse myself in it.

I don't "force" myself to revisit the sad feeling when my thoughts wander off, and I don't build momentum for the sad thoughts. I do cry. I do miss my siblings. I think about my mother and all my brothers' loved ones who miss them along with me. But I make sure to take deep breaths and I remind myself of how wonderful it is that we all love each other and are on good terms. I allow the thought train to keep moving forward and not linger at the sadness and grief station.

One of the things that keep the thought train moving forward is giving. Giving doesn't have to be grand. Even giving something small can activate the centers in the brain that make us feel joy and delight. An increasing number of studies find a neurological connection between giving, the activation of pleasure centers in the brain, and the production of oxytocin. Furthermore, oxytocin makes people give more generously, thus creating a neuro-biological cycle that keeps reactivating itself. Even the smallest act of giving can activate that cycle in our brains.

So, because I missed my brothers earlier today, I wrote a loving text message in our family messaging group, and let everyone know just how much I love them. Giving through a small text of love!

33. Giving Energy

This morning, I decided to treat myself to some fresh pastries. I drove to my favorite bakery to grab a cup of coffee and a croissant. On my way there, I saw an old man sitting on the sidewalk, begging.

I fumbled through my wallet and found one bill. I said to him: "Hang on, I'll get some change and come back." I bought my coffee and croissant, stepped outside, and gave him what change I had left. He was very happy, and I was even happier.

Sometimes, it seems that the hardest thing to do is to give money; yet sometimes, it's the easiest. Money is flowing energy; it's important that we let it ripple through us by giving and receiving.

How does giving money impact you? Is it easier to give money, or do you prefer other modes/ways of giving?

Welcome to the Portal

# of Acceptance

Welcome to the Portal of Acceptance

34. The Portal of Acceptance – A Tricky Portal

It would seem that accepting is the opposite of giving, but in fact, acceptance completes the act of giving because one cannot give if there's no one who can accept. Theoretically speaking, accepting or otherwise receiving should be quite easy for us. After all, accepting is agreeing to receive; it's practically passive. But the truth is that this is a very tricky portal. Acceptance is the ability to trust, or perhaps agree to trust those who give to us. In a way, accepting requires being momentarily helpless; it's realizing that we didn't or cannot decide what will happen next and simply accepting it.

Acceptance is about receiving things as well as accepting the way things are. It's way easier for us to give than accept. I am referring to actually accepting a hug, money, love, and all sorts of things. When we accept, we don't choose what we're given. When we succeed in accepting and allow ourselves to truly receive, we feel very happy.

The opposite of acceptance: The opposite of acceptance is control. When I struggle to trust and let go, I try to control and take what "I deserve." Therefore, the opposite of acceptance isn't giving – it's taking. When we don't believe that we will receive what we want we have the urge to become takers, which is motivated by our disbelief that we have our own share and that we'll get what we deserve too. So, acceptance allows us to enter a state of happiness and control or "taking" pushes us out of such a state.

Course of action: One of the things that helped me practice acceptance was deciding to stop exchanging gifts. In the past, when I'd receive a gift, I would always make sure that there was a gift receipt. I wanted to feel in control over what I was receiving. When I understood the wisdom behind acceptance, I decided that I wouldn't exchange gifts anymore. If I enjoy a present I received, I'll keep it and use it. If the present isn't right for me, I'll pass it forward to someone who can enjoy it. That was a great exercise in acceptance. It also freed up energy and time that I had otherwise spent in exchanging gifts.

35. The Universe has a GPS System, too. Use it.

The GPS system is my guardian angel.

True – it makes the occasional mistake. But ever since I started using it, I've become bolder when I drive places. I allow myself to make mistakes, take a wrong turn, or choose an alternative way because I know it's the app's responsibility to lead me to my destination. I can just enjoy the ride.

The same goes for life: Faith in a protective and benevolent force helps me conduct my life in a way that allows me to deeply explore all the little roads and side paths of my life. Ever since I've started to allow myself to believe that the universe is run by a higher force whose sole purpose is to help me reach the full potential of my life in the best way for me, I've been willing to believe that I can recover and even grow from deep pain or a bitter disappointment.

Believing in the good of the universe, in a force that always works in my favor, is the foundation of the portal of acceptance. According to the *Seven Portals of Happiness* approach, when I succeed in believing the universe's GPS is a benevolent force that wants only what's best for me, I can accept certain situations or events and can transform setbacks into benefits.

Then, it's much easier for me to feel happy even in complicated situations.

36. Allow Yourself to Accept

When I work in my clinic, I hear things like: "I don't know how to accept" or "all I do is give." The ability to accept is very important, and we don't always allow ourselves to practice this ability.

Why?

Because giving makes us feel capable, whereas accepting requires us to surrender. Acceptance forces the person who is accepting to trust the giver and believe that what they'll receive will be right for them. Accepting means admitting that I'm lacking. Accepting is an ability that allegedly makes us inferior. But when I learn to accept and surrender I allow abundance into my life. Nothing can come in if I'm unwilling to accept.

If you want to understand the role that acceptance plays in your life, try to think of how and where you accept in your life, and where you have trouble receiving.

37. The Art of Acceptance

As I've previously told you, many years ago, Odi and I decided to live in Australia for a couple of years. It was a well-calculated decision; we wanted to show our children that life can be lived differently. We felt that our life back home was perfect but adventureless. We felt that we deserved a family adventure that would spread our horizons and bring us closer as a unit. I was accepted into a PhD track in Melbourne and Odi received leave without pay from the airline company. We packed one suitcase for each of us, left behind a familiar home and large extended family, and set off on our Australian adventure.

Since Odi worked for an airline company and we could get extremely cheap flight tickets (though we had to fly standby), we decided we'd save some money on our tickets and place our trust in the Spirits of Adventure.

We arrived at the airport as two parents, four children, and five suitcases headed on a two-year adventure to the other side of the globe without any confirmed seats on the flight.

Flying standby is an art in and of itself: the art of listening to the universe's uncertainty, and being willing to "go with the flow;" or, in other words, the art of acceptance.

So, we sat at the airport and waited for a flight to Hong Kong, which was the only available connection to Melbourne back then. About an hour before takeoff, the flight captain, who was Odi's colleague, called him to apologize.

"I'm so sorry," he said, "but we only have one seat on the flight to Hong Kong, and you need six. There's nothing I can do."

At first, it felt like sprinting into a glass wall. It was something that we couldn't even see, but hit us hard all the same. We looked at each other, and I heard the wheels in Odi's head spin, twirl, and recalculate our route. "Listen," he told me, "there's a flight to Bangkok about thirty minutes after the flight to Hong Long. Maybe we should try and catch that one?"

"But there are no flights from Bangkok to Melbourne," I replied.

"Right, but there are flights to Sydney. Perhaps they'll agree to change our tickets to tickets from Bangkok to Sydney?"

We immediately headed to the airline's service point at the airport. They approved the exchange, and called the airline company in Bangkok on our behalf, asking them to approve the change too. Indeed, there's something magical about belonging to the family of international transportation! And so, we took our kids, made sure that the suitcases were rerouted, and instead of turning right and heading to Gate 8, we took a left and walked through Gate 6 on our way to our grand adventure. We arrived at Sydney and from there reached Melbourne. After a fifty-hour journey, we arrived at the empty house we rented, and fell asleep on the floor-to-floor carpet.

Our Australian period was one of the most beautiful and significant periods of our lives. It gave us everything we hoped for, and then some more. We made friends and saw things we couldn't have seen elsewhere. The most important part was that it was a long lesson in acceptance. Nothing we had planned happened as we had intended. And yet, the moment we surrendered and agreed to accept reality exceeded all expectations.

The more we agree to accept and let go, the happier we can be about the events that transpire, even when it seems that reality completely contradicts everything we wanted and planned. That is the art of acceptance.

38. What Was Taken from You? What Did You Receive?

At the beginning of 2021, I was listening to Lee Harris' Annual Energy Update. Harris is an intuitive and spiritual guide and teacher to whom I love to listen. He suggested that we write down the things that we've received from 2020 and the things we're letting go of and putting behind us in 2020.

Of course, I instantly knew what I left behind in 2020. In 2020 I lost my young brother, and I was giving up on his physical presence in my life. I was putting behind me long summer nights of us sitting together in the swimming pool, like two happy hippos, talking for hours about our kids, the world, life, and everything.

I had to give all that up – not by choice, but by acceptance. I would have to accept reality for what it is, and know that I will no longer have that relationship with my brother.

However, in 2020, I also realized that the method that I developed and teach is an amazing approach to a happy life. The *Seven Portal of Happiness* model is the gift I had received that same year. Developing it, and realizing the insights it introduced into my life, have practically helped and even saved me as I was going through that painful period in my life.

I've accepted amazing people including new students in my life, all of whom enjoy learning and thinking with me about how to deal with pain and struggles that are an inseparable part of our lives.

And despite all the pain and hardships, try and remember that behind it all, as the Israeli poet Yehuda Amichai said, lies great happiness.

What did you accept and what was taken from you this year?

39. "No Other Option" is a Fictional Concept

There are indeed periods in our private or collective lives when the events surrounding us challenge our ability to see things positively or maintain our internal happiness levels. Sometimes, the world blows a fuse, and then we all get electrocuted.

For instance, the climate crisis looming over us all, financial instability that suddenly runs rampant, global democracy hanging by a threat, and even our 'small' private world can undergo changes, uncertainty, transformations, and suffer pain and personal loss.

Feeling helpless is the worst thing when discussing happiness. In fact, anger is easier to transform into happiness than helplessness. The best way to handle helplessness is by first realizing and agreeing to feel it.

It sounds rather simple, but it isn't.

Helplessness is such a hard feeling that we tend to run away from it as quickly as possible. But if we take a deep breath and agree to accept helplessness, we can start climbing out of the metaphoric pit.

Practically speaking, what does that mean?

It means realizing that because of the helplessness we feel bad and experience anger, guilt, victimization, and so on. Once we agree to accept that feeling of helplessness, we can remember that we're never truly helpless. In every situation, we can choose what to do and how to react.

If I'm afraid to join a protest because of police brutality, I choose to stay home. It's still a choice, and it's completely legitimate.

If I choose to keep doing something that is forbidden according to my current reality, like hiding Jews during WWII, that's a choice too, and it's also entirely legitimate.

Frankly, regardless of what we choose to do, as long as we remember that we always have a choice and that the prospect of "no choice" is actually a myth that we and others hold onto, we won't feel as helpless. The less helpless we feel, the closer we will bring ourselves to feel happiness. This is exactly what I'm here to prove.

Q.E.D.

NOT MY BEST VERSION

Sometimes, when we experience hardships, the most important thing we can do is agree to surrender and allow the pain, helplessness, and sadness to simply exist, and to accept the irreversibility of the situation.

Most importantly, if we try to take action motivated by our acceptance of the pain and fall into the pit of self-victimization, then we should simply be empathetic to ourselves.

We shouldn't self-criticize for not being the best version of ourselves in the current situation. Instead, we should know that sometimes we can't be the best version of ourselves. And that's okay, too.

40. We Are All One Fabric of Consciousness

Recently, I've been undergoing a purification process, where I've been trying to be precise and shed unnecessary layers I've gathered throughout my life. I understand that I am who I am because that is my contribution to the greater fabric that is in fact the unison of the Creator/Universe/source. I haven't settled on one name because the essence of creation conveys a multifaceted name, and I accept that.

I've recently realized that I remember many of my reincarnations; however, in none of those reincarnations that I know of (except my current one and perhaps a very ancient one) have I been Jewish. That made me grasp something very essential about myself and my mission here with this time on earth. I'm here to connect truths of different and varied sources into one absolute truth, into a texture of different shapes and patterns that creates cohesion.

In my current reincarnation, my roots are deeply grounded in Jewish scholarship. I've always known and learned Judaism, and these past years, I dove deep while learning Rabbi Nachman's discipline, reading the wisdom of the sages of the Mishna and the Talmud, and of course, delving into Kabbalah. All this study has been done regardless of any religious establishment.

I was fascinated to discover that the wisdom of Zen, Esther Hicks teachings, Louise Hay's abundance methodology, the Gnosticism of the ancient Christians, and other philosophies of researchers such as Graham Hancock, Gregg Braden, Bruce Lipton, and Joe Dispenza are all different facets of the same truth.

I'm in the process of implementing that truth deeply inside of me. The Kabballah language sits well with the terminology I use, perhaps because all my teachers currently speak the language of Kabbalah in some form or another.

I've spent decades fighting and negotiating the great anger I had felt, and I couldn't understand it's origin. Now, things are clearer. The moment I agreed to feel, understand, and admit that I don't exist solely on a physical level in this world, but that I also exist on a spiritual level, I was able to release the pain that existed in my body for many decades.

Today, when I find myself upset, I try not to let anger control my behavior nor my thoughts. I placate myself, and make peace with the world while doing everything in my power to transmute my anger into insights that can elevate me spiritually.

I feel and believe that all humankind, animals, plants, and even inanimate objects are connected and are all expressions of the same fabric of consciousness of the universe. When I succeed in understanding and feeling just that, my life becomes so much better.

Thus, I observe everything that happens to me – whether good or not – as a message from my inner self about my level of aware connectedness in every given moment.

41. Sometimes, the Universe Works Through Surprising Messengers

Acceptance is a form of listening to the universe. On the one hand, it's about surrendering to the events transpiring around us. On the other, it's our willingness to admit to ourselves what our true desire is and on yet another, it's our acceptance of fulfilling our desire. There are probably many other aspects, but these will suffice for now.

So, let me tell you what happened to me. The universe spoke to me, loud and clear.

Author Yuval Abramovitz offered gifts in celebration of his *The List* book series' anniversary. One of the gifts was a discount for his writing workshop. I really wanted to sign up, but had previous engagements for that date. So, I let it go, and the discount expired.

Then, I was told that my previous engagement was delayed, and Yuval also decided to renew the discount for the writing workshop for twenty-four hours.

I nodded to the universe, and immediately signed up and attended.

The workshop was amazing. A great thank you to Yuval and *The List* team. I learned important content while being surrounded by a pleasant group, and the experience was fun and empowering. At the end of the workshop, Yuval said that I had to write. I replied that I was trying.

"Don't try – just write!" he said determinedly.

On my way back home from the workshop, I toyed with the idea, still thrilled by the experience I had.

What should I write?

Perhaps I want to do it, but what and why would I?

As I was driving and considering the idea of writing, I received a call from an unknown number.

"Omna?"

"Yes?"

"This is Michael from the local news. Could you please send us your email address?"

"Sure, Michael, could you please explain what for?"

"Yes, we would like you to write a piece for the newspaper."

So apparently, when I listen, the universe speaks to me. All I have to do is accept.

42. Sometimes, Accepting "No" is the Right Thing to Do

As previously mentioned, a little over a decade ago, while I was writing my PhD dissertation in Australia, my beloved brother fell ill, and we returned back home in the middle of my studies. It was the smartest and best decision I've made in my entire life.

One of the things that helped me get through that painful and grief-ridden time was Victoria University's willingness to help, support, and allow me to finish writing, all while fully knowing that I was staying in my home country.

Recently, I've been thinking how random it was that I ended up writing my PhD at Victoria University of all places, and how important it was for me to accept the way things turned out and how those turns worked in my favor during the unexpected hard times that followed.

I was planning on completing my PhD at Monash University, a prestigious university in Melbourne. I negotiated with their gender studies department for months. Each time, they asked me to bring more documents, more proposals, more diplomas, and whatnot. Suddenly, one bright Friday morning, three days before Odi and I were supposed to fly to Melbourne to find a house to live in for the next two years and schools for four children, I received an email from Monash University. The email said that of the three potential supervisors, one was taking a sabbatical, the second was going on a year-long research expedition in India, and the third wasn't interested in my research topic. Therefore, they rejected my application.

However, it wasn't just my education on the line. Our family visa to Australia depended on my admission. It was Friday, and we were supposed to fly off on Sunday. I won't bore you with all the details about how I found a university that offers PhD studies in my field of psychotherapy who admitted me, but then I revealed that it was the only one out of 300 educational institutions in Melbourne that couldn't provide us with a visa. After extensively exploring the internet, I found Victoria University and applied for an art diploma that made us all eligible for a visa. Two and a half years later, I submitted my PhD dissertation in gender studies to Victoria University. Their staff truly did everything in their power to support me during that time, and enabled me, against all odds, to complete my research, write my dissertation, and receive my degree.

This story is but one example of how the so-called blows we receive along the way can in fact be the universe's way of directing us to our right path. When we left for Australia, we couldn't imagine, even in our worst dreams, that my brother would get sick and we'd have to return earlier than expected. I didn't know that I wouldn't be accepted into the university I wanted due to reasons that had nothing to do with me. However, I ended up at the only university that was right for me which helped me through my hardships. I think quite a lot about the messages I've received from the universe throughout the years and how I've learned to attentively listen to them, and not only roll with them or work against them when I thought that my path should have been different. I know that this ability I've developed – the ability to attentively and actively listen to the universe – is the essence of the portal of acceptance and has improved my life in every possible aspect and made me a happier person.

43. Sometimes, What Appears to be a Compromise is, in Fact, Great Love

My mother grows tomatoes.

No, she doesn't do it for a living, but she does it with a lot of love.

My mother is almost ninety years old. As a part of her professional career, she studied biology at Tel Aviv University. Actually, her dream was to study math; however, they hadn't opened the math department at the university at the time, and she couldn't afford to move to a different city. Therefore, she chose the only scientific program available at Tel Aviv: biology. Later, she taught biology for four decades.

A couple of years ago, my mother became a balcony farmer. A beautiful squash seduced her into fiddling with its seeds. And BAM she had a crop of squash displayed in her living room.

After the squash came the tomatoes.

That time a luscious tomato flirted with her and my mom collected its seeds, cleaned, dried, sowed, planted, gathered, and moved it to bigger pots... and BAM she had a small field of tomatoes.

My mother uses all the knowledge she learned about sixty years ago at the biology department to grow her vegetables – the same knowledge she had taught her students for dozens of years. She recognizes female and male flowers and pollinates one pistil instead of another. That way, she makes sure her plants produce fruits, and she also enjoys the analysis and use of her rich experience in the field.

My mother loves her tomatoes; A lot. She waters them, covers them in plastic wrap when the weather gets stormy, and checks on them several times a day.

What can we learn from this story?

Sometimes, it might seem that life pushed us toward a certain direction that we didn't want. However, if we wait patiently, feel grateful, and remember to find the positive in every situation, we'll often find that what appears to be a mistake is in fact something we actually love dearly and were unaware of.

Welcome to the Portal

of Gratitude

Welcome to the Portal of Gratitude

44. The Portal that Teaches Us the Wisdom to be Grateful for What is

Gratitude allows us to see the good in our lives – as it is right now. When I focus on gratitude, I adjust my gaze to see the good rather than focus on what isn't good. It's all about focusing on the solution and not on the problem. Studies show that people who keep a daily gratitude journal can alleviate their depression. Writing down things you're grateful for improves your mental state.

Many people are reluctant to be grateful for the positive things in their lives because they're afraid that expressing their gratitude will reinforce their current situation and prevent something better from coming. But that isn't true. In fact, if I'm grateful for what I have, the frequency that resonates inside me draws me to experience things that will make me grateful again, leading to even better experiences. The more positive things I find about my current situation and the more often I express gratitude, the more positive my outlook is and more positive things will come into focus.

The other side: However, the other side of gratitude, the side that pushes us away from happiness, is dissatisfaction and grievances. It is finding reasons to be displeased and dissatisfied, asking why I don't receive what I deserve. It is wondering why things are the way they are, and why can't I ever catch a break. One might think that when we're dissatisfied, we might improve the situation; however, that's not how things work. Complaining increases dissatisfaction and distances us from happiness.

Course of action: Pay attention to when we start to complain and keep ourselves from slipping into a state of dissatisfaction. Naturally, we all need to vent from time to time and it's important to blow off steam, but the less we dwell on it and the quicker we return to look at the positive and refocus on gratitude, the better we'll feel and our levels of happiness will intensify.

45. Let's Talk Research

Gratitude improves our health. People who are grateful experience less pain and generally report better health conditions at all ages. Of course, we could assume that people who feel well have an easier time being grateful. However, there's a growing body of research that suggests that when people introduce gratitude into their lives on a daily basis, their health improves.

Gratitude frees us from toxic feelings including jealousy, resentment, and frustration. It has a positive impact on our levels of happiness and subjective well-being.

Gratitude increases empathy and reduces aggression.

People who are grateful tend to be more sociable, empathetic, and kind even to people who aren't as sociable. A study conducted in 2012, showed that people who scored higher on the gratitude scale were less resentful when they received negative feedback. They were more sensitive and caring towards others, and weren't as inclined to take revenge. They exhibited compassion and forgiveness.

Gratitude allows us to sleep better. According to a study from 2016, subjects who dedicated 15 minutes every evening to recording in their gratitude journal have improved their quality of sleep.Gratitude also improves our sense of self-worth.

Gratitude causes a reduction in social comparisons, thus contributing to the improvement of our self-esteem. Instead of resenting others for having more money, better jobs, or being thinner, gratitude allows us to appreciate the positive in others, see their virtues and how well they treat us, and thus avoid comparing. In fact, gratitude prevents us from hurting ourselves due to the positive feelings we have towards who we are.

Gratitude reinforces mental strength. Studies show that gratitude reduces stress and helps people overcome trauma. Research conducted in 2006 that studied Vietnam veterans found that the higher their gratitude levels were, the less they suffered from PTSD. Two studies from 2003 have found that people's ability to recover from 9/11 was stronger the more grateful they were. When I recognize what I can be grateful for – even in hard times – my ability to withstand trauma is stronger.

We all have the ability to increase our gratitude. The

more we minimize our complaints and dissatisfaction and find things, people, and events that we can be grateful for, the more we will improve the quality of our lives. Gratitude is a simple and available way to improve our subjective well-being.

46. Now, Let's Talk About Miracles

When we think about miracles, we tend to imagine something supernatural: a sea parted in half, a mother who lifted a car that trapped her baby, or a lioness nursing a lamb. But if we stop and look around us, we'll soon find out that our very existence on this planet is a miracle.

The fact that one avocado seed can grow into a full tree bearing dozens of avocados every year is enough of a phenomenon to be called a miracle – the way I see it.

The fact that water – which is essential to our existence – simply pours down from the skies, that oxygen exists, and that trees produce oxygen for us as they clean the air from carbon dioxide, is nothing less than a miracle.

I mean to say that our very existence on this planet is a miracle and the more we realize and appreciate that fact, the more we can cherish our lives the way they are and be grateful.

And gratitude creates happiness.

47. Why is Gratitude a Genetic Contradiction?

We're biologically and genetically designed to seek out danger and to search for what might be wrong. Why?

There are two types of mistakes that we can make. The first is thinking there's a problem and that there's danger where there isn't. Then, we react as if there is some danger, and we might deprive ourselves of something which results in physical stress. We put ourselves in an uncomfortable situation that might even physically hurt us, but it won't kill us that very instant. If I think there's danger, and I'm careful where I shouldn't be, the fear creates discomfort, but it doesn't kill me.

On the other hand, the other type of mistake we make is thinking there isn't any danger when there is. That mistake can only be made once. Because, if I thought there were no tigers in the bushes and I was wrong, that mistake cannot be corrected.

In other words, genetically, as a life-saving mechanism, we're supposed to be looking for "what's wrong" in the world around us, rather than looking for "what's right."

However, in the modern world, that tendency causes many issues. The fewer tigers lurking in the bushes, the more energy we waste in vain over worrying or being dissatisfied. Sometimes we even make ourselves ill with unnecessary concerns.

Our natural tendency to look for flaws in order to protect our lives often forms "negative comraderies." Comraderies are human beings' best shields. We're stronger when we're unified. We're stronger because we're able to form a large and communicative group in order to exist in a world that doesn't always work in our favor. Therefore, once it is paired with the force of comradery, the mechanism of "let's see what is wrong in the world around us," creates a powerful, protective, and significant defense, which is very difficult to change.

On the other hand, gratitude rewires our brains and allows us to change our biological mechanism that seeks to find flaws into a new mechanism that finds the positive in every situation. Keeping a gratitude journal contradicts our natural tendency to focus on the negative, seemingly to protect our very existence. Looking for the negative may have worked in a world filled with daily dangers, such as predators and natural catastrophes, but in the modern world, that tendency is more of an obstacle than a benefit. Therefore, the more we practice working against that biological tendency and instead look for the positive and be grateful for it, the more we will adjust ourselves to the world we currently live in rather than the world that formulated our biology.

48. On Chutes and Ladders

One of the things that help me preserve my positive outlook is gratitude. When I feel in despair, lose all hope, and gracefully slip into a state of self-pity, gratitude is like a rope ladder that dangles right in front of me.

Though I'd love to take credit for it, gratitude is a well-known tool; some might even say an ancient one. Every religion teaches us to be grateful for what we have, and even for what we have yet to receive. That being said, it's not always easy to feel grateful.

If we momentarily return to my story, lying there in the pit of desperation and victimhood, sometimes, gratitude is a steady and solid ladder nailed to the wall, and all I need to do is climb it. However, occasionally, gratitude is a rickety rope ladder, hanging a little over my head, and I need to work hard to climb it. Perhaps I need to raise myself in order to free myself from the pit.

But either way, once I start looking for the positive and remain satisfied with what is and thankful for it, I'm on my way up the ladder and out of the pit.

49. A Celebration of Gratitude

The one thing most of the world knows about Thanksgiving is that the following day is Black Friday, which is also the harbinger of the Christmas craze. People might also be familiar with the stuffed turkey, which is an important part of Thanksgiving dinner.

People aren't as familiar with the fact that Thanksgiving is a holiday centered around gratitude. The holiday was established by American pioneers – former Europeans who arrived on the American continent and decided to make it their new home. They felt grateful for all the abundance that the new continent had to offer them.

Discussing the horrible ramifications of the complexities of European colonialism is beyond the scope of this book, yet I would like to focus on the fabulous idea of dedicating an entire holiday to celebrating what is, and being fully grateful for it. That is the true meaning of Thanksgiving.

Saying 'thank you' is being polite; it makes our shared lives together more pleasant. However, being thankful is a state of mind; it enables us to feel joyous and fortunate for what is at a deep soul level. Being thankful is feeling our hearts swell with joy when we see beautiful flowers, or when we're mesmerized by gorgeous clouds.

Gratitude is one of the most important paths leading us to a life of happiness. When we're grateful, our brains form new neurological routes that allow us to feel more positive; they allow us to feel positive emotions such as joy and love, and therefore, experience our day-to-day more positively.

Gratitude, whether for something specific or as a general feeling, expands our ability to feel happiness in the long run.

When do you express gratitude for what you have in your life?

50. Daily Gratitude Increases Happiness

As I've previously mentioned, my mother is almost 90 and I'm proud to say it, because I don't take it for granted. As my mother puts it: She spent her childhood playing catch with the Nazis throughout Europe.

They didn't catch her.

My mother loves creating. I think I got it from her. She's an expert at cooking and an excellent writer, and her favorite thing is to take seeds of things and turn them into plants. So, she had forests of avocados and yams in her living room and kombucha mushrooms that she's been growing for many years.

I already told you how a few years ago, when she was still a young maiden at 85, she sliced a gorgeous squash, and decided that such a perfect squash deserves continuity. Using those white seeds – the ones we roast or add to a salad – she created a bunch of beautiful plants. My mother was grateful. She told me that she felt those small saplings were like a new life, sprouting in her heart. She wanted to nurture the sense of wonder and gratitude they had awakened in her.

So, we visited a gardening nursery and bought her three large planters and my mama turned into a balcony farmer. Every morning, she'd go to her balcony and talk to her plants, water and pollinate them as needed, and watch them grow and flourish. These days, her growing endeavors have grown, and she's taken over the entire balcony. The plants make her very happy, and she's thankful for them every day.

51. Listening Inwardly Allows Us to Feel Grateful

I don't like noise. I'm overwhelmed when I find myself in noisy places, surrounded by loud music and people talking all at once. I enjoy talking to the people around me. Therefore, when I found out that the best way to talk to people in a noisy place was to lean in and whisper, I was happy to adopt that practice. I consider it to be an actual technique, because whispering isn't a natural instinct for me.

Sometimes, my life feels like a crowded place, and the sounds surrounding me are others' voices worrying me and shouting about how dangerous the world is. Or perhaps it's even the media, telling me about injustices, violence, and pain.

And then I lean into myself and try to listen to my inner self whispering to me, or small and hushed messages that the universe sends my way.

One of the things that I seek inside, especially when it's loud outside, is focusing on the positive and finding what I want to be grateful for. The more attuned I am to listening to the whispers of gratitude and repeating them out loud to myself and others, the more I discover that life is actually amazing.

52. The Universe Loves Gratitude

Let me share with you a story told by the author Jen Sincero. Let's say you've baked cookies and you've decided to share them with your neighbors. Some of the neighbors take the cookies and say, "Oh, that's very nice of you, thank you." Some take the cookies without saying a word. Others refuse the cookies and say, "Ugh, no, thank you. I'm watching my weight. I don't eat sugar and gluten; I hate cookies." However, there's one kid who always says: "Thank you for the cookies. They were really delicious. Please let me know next time you make a batch. I would love to help you, or learn how to make them." Next time we bake cookies, who would we want to share them with?

The universe works in a similar way. If you're having a tough time with the universe, you can address your mind. The mind – that psychological entity that manages us – also thrives on gratitude. Why? Because gratitude gives us pleasure. It makes us feel meaningful. When someone thanks me, I feel meaningful; I feel that my actions, or even my existence – mean something to someone. Our mind's main purpose is to push us away from pain and bring us closer to pleasure.

The more grateful we are, the more we develop gratitude as a habit and build new neurological paths in our brain, which in turn allow us to feel more pleasure, decrease harmful stress levels, and see the world as a better and more pleasant place to live in.

Therefore, gratitude is a portal to happiness.

53. Why Should Each and Every One of Us Start Our Lives with Gratitude?

Throughout the years, I've met quite a few amazing, strong, good, interesting, loving, warm, and generous women, and some who weren't. Over time, I realized the huge impact one woman had on my life and the person I am.

My mother.

I know there's been extensive discussion about the importance of normalizing families of different types. I believe this to be a positive step in the right direction. I think that the more family types we have, the better chance children have of growing in a loving and supportive environment. The more men believe that parenthood is also their right and not just women's domain, the more children will have loving parents and humanity as a whole will benefit. This is purely in everyone's best interest.

I was lucky enough to have two loving parents who wanted nothing but the best for me and my siblings.

True, they made mistakes along the way. But who doesn't?

A great part of my own growth happened thanks to my parents' mistakes, so I'm grateful to them for that too.

And still, I would like to thank my mother.

Naturally, women aren't obligated to give birth or even raise a child in order to "be a woman." That being said, humanity as a whole, without exceptions, owes thanks to the woman who carried them in their womb long enough for them to be born. It's a simple biological event, but perhaps the most important of all. Pregnancy might not be an illness, but it certainly isn't an easy thing, and neither is childbirth. Each and every one of us has received that gift from one woman: the right to be born into this world. We haven't even started talking about the years of nurturing and care that we receive after we are born, all for the purpose of allowing us to survive and exist.

So, yes, I believe that we all owe thanks to our mothers, for their willingness to be pregnant and give birth so that we can live. I would also like to express my gratitude to all women, those whom I have met along the way and those who were good to me. But first and foremost, I thank my mother for bringing me into this world.

Thank you, Mommy.

Welcome to the Portal

of Compassion

Welcome to the Portal of Compassion

54. The Portal of Compassion: The Portal that Minimizes Criticism in Your Life

What is compassion? I'd like to offer a fresh perspective on the term compassion. Compassion is accepting myself and others just the way we are. Compassion is the realization that we're all basically human. Thus we might make mistakes, disappoint or hurt others – including the people we love – because we're not perfect, and we're not supposed to be in any way. This is how it should be and it's fine.

The opposite of compassion: The opposite of compassion is criticism, which can also manifest as judgment, competitiveness, and pity. When I say something like "She's so amazing. I'll never be as amazing," I'm being critical and judgmental because I'm judging both of us, deciding that she's better than I am, and criticizing myself. But if I say something like: "She's such an inspiration for running a marathon. I want that too," that isn't criticism.

Course of action: Every time I have a critical thought, such as: "How can she wear that at her age, size, or anything else," or: "Why can't I get there on time? Why do I always have to be late?" I stop and say to myself: "Why shouldn't she wear that if it makes her happy?" or "Everyone can be late from time to time, and I'm doing my best to make it on time."

Thus I start answering the countless judgmental voices in my head. The more I pay attention to my own critical voice about myself and others, and the more I learn to reply to that voice while understanding and believing that we're all human and doing our best; I flex my compassion muscle. Then, living in this world becomes a happier experience and more pleasant.

55. Compassion is Self-Love

Loving ourselves allows us to shed light on the dark places within us. These places that often unconsciously – and many times unsuccessfully – guide our actions.

Self-love is a light that brightens our darkest corners, because we're willing to love ourselves, warts and all. The more light there is within me, the more I understand what it is I'm doing and the reason behind it. This process reduces the rejected parts within us that in fact govern us under the auspices of our inner subconscious darkness.

So, if you think self-love is about boasting and unjustifiably flaunting that you're the best, you've got it wrong, my friend. It's very much the opposite!

Loving yourself means realizing that perfection is nonexistent, and therefore, shouldn't be an aspiration. It means that you understand that you can try to correct any mistake, and you can always apologize, but self-hatred and unforgiving self-criticism are not a necessary part of the correction process.

Self-love is about realizing and discovering our own humanity which cannot and will not be perfect. It's the foundation of being human, and therefore, we should learn to forgive ourselves out of compassion and empathy. Self-love is the true secret that will assist us in bringing anything we want into our lives; it enables us to understand and be compassionate towards ourselves and everyone else.

56. Compassion. Not Pity.

Last Yom Kippur, I started pondering: "What is the difference between compassion and pity?"

Seemingly, those two words are synonymous. Pity by definition is identifying with another and acknowledging their pain or trouble. "Being there for someone" is the modern iteration with which we can connect to this concept. However, even if we feel the other's pain in the sincerest and deepest way, when we pity someone, we distance ourselves from them. When we pity someone else, it means we feel superior to them and might even criticize the subject of our pity. When we feel sorry for someone or pity them, it means we consider them to be lesser than us, and by doing so, we engage in comparison, competition, and criticism.

Compassion, on the other hand, is the foundational realization that we're both the same and therefore, the core of compassion is love and acceptance. Compassion also means that we understand that if we're doing well and the other isn't, the tables might turn at any given moment. Pity, however, is always a feeling one has when they're in a position of power. This is not to say that there's anything inherently wrong with it. However, pity can quite easily affect our perspective, and lead us to see the other as an unfortunate individual. By pitying others, we rob the other of their agency and engage in victimhood. That is also why some people say, "don't feel sorry for me, I don't need it." We all know people who express their love by feeling sorry for others, but that love comes at a price; it creates a sense of victimhood for the person being pitied.

Seeing as love and acceptance are at the heart of compassion, the difference between compassion and pity is significant with regard to the way we treat others, and it is even more significant with regard to the way we treat ourselves. When we feel sorry for ourselves, we reinforce our own misery and deepen aspects of victimhood within our self-perception. This form of victimhood in fact weakens us, because we feel helpless in the face of our circumstances or the people who had wronged us.

On the other hand, when we're compassionate towards ourselves, we understand that very much like other people, we're not perfect. By accepting this imperfection, we take responsibility for our own circumstances, without any unnecessary guilt, self-judgment, or criticism. Compassion allows us to accept our imperfections, mistakes, small or big failures, and even self-pity as a part of our own humanity. When we're compassionate towards ourselves, we can redirect our energy to handle the situation at hand. This is the true power of compassion; which makes it a significant portal on our happiness journey.

57. And Then May Said: You Gotta Write About it in Your Book!

"Write what?" I asked.

"That thing you just explained to me. That's a thought that has to make it into the book. That's what you have to write for people to understand how the portals of happiness actually work."

So, as per her request, this is what happened:

May and I were working on a new product – one of many we've been developing for the **HappinesSkool** community, and the hours went by. May asked for a cup of coffee. I made her a cup of coffee with oat milk – just the way she liked it. I also gave her a couple of pieces of my favorite chocolate.

Since we were talking about forgiveness, May said: "I'm trying real hard not to apologize for bothering you with my coffee. Is that the portal of forgiveness?"

"Not really," I replied. "That's the portal of compassion."

You don't want to apologize because you've done something bad, but rather because you're criticizing yourself for having bothered me. Silencing that criticism is being compassionate, and therefore, it's the portal of compassion; agreeing to enjoy your coffee and chocolate is the portal of acceptance. Allowing me to pamper you is the portal of giving, which makes me overjoyed, and this is the portal of joy."

Happiness lies in our relationships with other people and ourselves, and the more we follow the seven-portal map, the better our relationships will be, as well as our daily happiness levels.

58. Compassion, Spice and Everything Nice

I'm a sucker for animated films, especially Disney and Pixar. Generally speaking, animated films warm my heart. One of my favorites is Ratatouille. If you haven't heard of it, it's about a French rat who watches a cooking show and dreams of becoming a Michelin-star chef.

Now, here's a secret about me so I hope you keep it to yourselves: I'm absolutely terrified of rats. I mean, standing-in-the-street-and-screaming kind of terrified. And yet, Ratatouille is one of my favorite movies, and I think I must have seen it dozens of times.

So, what makes me overcome my fear and watch this movie over and over again?

Ratatouille is a movie about compassion.

The "bad guy" in the movie is a food critic. In other words, a person who turned his razor-sharp ability to criticize into his bread and butter, which became an inseparable and essential part of his personality. That man doesn't possess a shred of compassion. He arrives at the restaurant where Remi the rat cooks in complete secrecy, only to stab his mighty pen at the tiniest of flaws.

Sometimes, we think that if we don't pass judgment, it means we're "less than" others. It is as if we're admitting that we're not smart enough to notice the flaws in our own circumstances. The reason why food critics or art critics often become celebrities and are admired is that we appreciate criticism more than compassion. When we're insecure about ourselves or our worth, the easiest and quickest way to boost our self-esteem is to criticize others. When we criticize another person, we feel better about ourselves. This happens for two reasons: First, as previously mentioned, our culture idolizes criticism, and second, if others aren't the best, then we can stop demanding perfection from ourselves.

Unfortunately, that's not how things work. Criticizing others all the time also makes us believe that we're being looked at and constantly criticized. It also increases the impact of our self-criticism. The more we criticize, the less happy we feel; because we find fault in everything, everyone, and ourselves. However, when we're compassionate to ourselves and others, when we accept that imperfection around us and in ourselves is beautiful and an inseparable part of humanity and earthliness, we can be happier with what is.

In the end, our beloved rat prepares a dish rich with flavors of love and childhood memories, which allows the critic to reconnect with his humanity and transforms him into a compassionate and loving person. Ego, the food critic, partners with the rat and his two human companions, and they open a modest and non-pretentious restaurant where they serve delicious food that evokes childhood memories in its diners and reminds us that we're all human – even if we're rats.

59. How Criticism (Doesn't) Serve Us?

Some might claim that criticism is driven by a desire to improve and be improved. This is also known as "constructive criticism." Well, I've got news for you; there is no such thing as constructive criticism. There's only destructive criticism. I should note that I acknowledge the importance of analyzing, processing, and drawing conclusions in a process as a whole, and yet, criticism is always destructive. Why?

Criticism is one of our society's major problems. It stems from insecurity. Criticism is judgmental and is derived from a hierarchical order that defines what is good, what isn't, and what is worse. People use criticism when they feel inadequate. People criticize others in order to feel better about themselves. Criticism is occasionally perceived as wise and superior to compliments or compassion. But it isn't.

Criticism is about policing ourselves and others out of fear – a fear of losing our place in a certain group. One might criticize themselves and claim that it's their way of improving themselves. We tend to say things to ourselves such as: "This isn't good enough. I didn't get it right again. I can't believe I'm late again." Sometimes, we even add a pejorative. But saying those things won't help us become better; in fact, it only makes us feel insecure about ourselves and our abilities.

The more I criticize myself and others, the more certain I am that everyone does it. Criticizing others also makes us believe that everyone is criticizing us. Thus, it leads to two reactions: first, relentless self-criticism. Secondly, it prevents us from allowing our inner voice to guide us because we're afraid that if we don't fit in, someone might criticize us. Then, we find ourselves living our lives and believing that everything we do, say, wear, or eat is being scrutinized, which results in anxiety and an inability to experience happiness.

As I've previously explained, compassion is the opposite of criticism. This is because I understand nothing is perfect, and so, I stop looking for perfection. This point is worth emphasizing because it's one of the most important things we can do on our journey of happiness. Once I am willing to accept myself, with all my shortcomings and mistakes, I accept my own humanity and behave compassionately toward myself. When I'm willing to acknowledge the fact that I am good enough just the way I am, I don't stop trying to improve myself – which is what most of us fear – but rather, I stop using self-hatred. The less I hate myself, the less I need to prove to myself that others aren't as good. Consequently, this reduces my criticism of others and increases my compassion inwardly and outwardly. Therefore, the more compassionate I am towards myself and others, and the less I criticize myself and others, the closer I am to happiness and my happiness levels increase.

60. We Criticize Because We're Afraid We Won't Belong

If there's one thing I hate, it's when people jokingly say: women are always mean to each other.

It infuriates me every single time. Why, you ask?

Because it implies that women harshly criticize other

women due to an inherent competitiveness that women possess among themselves, and not because of their position in a patriarchal society. What do I mean by that?

Women are policed in a patriarchal culture in numerous ways: Their clothes, their speech, the register of their laughter, when and where they go... There's hardly an aspect of women's everyday life that isn't being monitored and scrutinized as either moral or immoral.

If a woman is believed to have derailed from the moral codes for women, she is severely punished and is deemed either a slut or a bitch. One of the more widely-known aspects of this phenomenon is victim blaming. To this day, some cultures and societies physically punish women who stray from social conventions; sometimes, women even pay with their lives.

In order to maintain their position in their group, and to defend themselves from being persecuted, women have developed defense mechanisms, which includes criticizing themselves and other women. As a result, women aren't compassionate toward themselves and other women, even if those women are their daughters or sisters. Quite the contrary, the closer and more loving the relationship, the more the criticism is perceived to be a form of protection of the loved one.

One of the most critical expressions of the lack of compassion is the surge in eating disorders over the last fifty years. Ninety percent of women have some form of eating disorder! Eating disorders are a severe and compassionless form of self-criticism that essentially implies that a said woman or girl does not answer to social expectations of slimming down and minimizing herself as part of the definition of her femininity. Any woman who, God forbid, allows herself to eat as she pleases, or be anything but thin, is subject to criticism by other women who do conform to that model of femininity and who find it important to be part of the group or the community. Thus, self-criticizing and criticizing other women is a mechanism that preserves one's association with the group. However, since we've already mentioned that criticism is the opposite of compassion, and since the foundation of compassion is realizing we're all human, we can conclude that this relentless criticism undermines our humanity, and by doing so, not only distances us from happiness, but practically makes us constantly suffer.

61. Mothers and Daughters – Is it a Compassionless Relationship?

The most complicated relationship in our lives as women is the one we have with our mother or with our daughters – if we are lucky enough to have them. For centuries, the figure of mothers was split (very much like in fairy tales): the good, "biological" mother who dies when her daughter is very young, versus the evil "stepmother" who raises the daughter. This split is anything but "natural." It's one of the most effective policing instruments that patriarchy has created, and as a result, most of us police or restrict our daughters. It stems from our realization that we must protect and save our girls from "wolves" who might harm them. This mechanism has caused a rift in the most powerful relationship to have ever existed: the mother-daughter relationship.

And why is it the most powerful relationship?

Because women are powerful creatures.

When I use the word "powerful" I don't mean it in as in violent and aggressive, but rather in a way that conveys the strength that lies within us and allows us to move forward while overcoming obstacles and hardships. Once this power is reinforced by love, it becomes the most powerful force in the world. This is exactly the force the patriarchy has undermined for thousands of years, transforming the mother-daughter bond from a powerful and loving relationship into a compassionless and criticizing relationship. And why? Because we're afraid that this is our only means of protecting our daughters.

Splitting every mother into a good biological one and an evil stepmother has become a dominant practice in human culture for far too long. Even the biblical story about Sarah, Hagar, and Ishmael loosely touches upon the matter. I'd like to share with you how happy I was about a decade ago when I realized that this preconception has started to shatter.

These changes in collective consciousness often start in children's movies of all places. This newfound message first appeared in Disney's 2012 movie "Brave." The movie tells the story of a Disney princess and her relationship with her mother. Their relationship turns sour when the mother tries to force her daughter to live according to the world's conventions: be pretty, passive, and marriageable (because that should be every young girl's ultimate aspiration). The daughter rebels against her mother and plagues her mother with a curse. However, in the end, she manages to rectify the damage she has done. Both realize that the love they share is their true power and thus, they shatter the demands that essentially diminish their very essence, that is that marriage is the epitome of women's sole self-realization.

Yesterday, I coincidentally watched a movie and a TV show. Although they were seemingly different, both in fact approached a similar topic differently. The TV show is called "Ms. Marvel" and the protagonist is a teen girl who turns into a superhero. The movie I watched is called "Everything, Everywhere, All at Once," and is about the multiverse theory. However, the core of these movies revolves around the mother-daughter relationship and its rectification. Even when the mother is presented as judgmental and tough, the plot's agenda is to explain that the mother is only trying to protect her daughter in the way she has been taught, and she is not acting out of a lack of compassion. I left the movie theater yesterday in tears because I realized the change is finally here.

When our collective culture acknowledges that we're whole women, that we're allowed to feel sexy in a bikini and still be good mothers, and although we've all experienced some kind of sexual harassment we still believe injustice can be corrected, we can start to see the light at the end of the tunnel. Yes, we still have a long way to go. However, I can take a deep breath and practically feel the compassion and acceptance of our own humanity slowly seeping into our collective culture. I can tell that despite everything happening around us, we're heading towards a better tomorrow.

62. Compassion Allows Us to Move from Criticism to a Bird's Eye View

Last night we drove to a shiva. The father of our dear friend Ori passed away, and we wanted to embrace our friend in his difficult time.

We sat with Ori and his family for some time, and when we got up to leave, I took my phone and got into the car. When we arrived home, I left the car and searched for the purse, only to realize that I had forgotten my purse at Ori's place, which was about a 40-minute drive away.

So, the first thing I did was confirm that it was indeed there. After that, the first thought that crossed my mind was: How could I have been so stupid and careless?

In the past, I would have probably been very angry at myself, expressing my disappointment at my mistake that would consequently force me to add a 90-minute drive to my already-busy schedule. However, this time, I didn't berate myself. Instead, I quietly said to myself, "Okay, you made a mistake." Then I replied, "But I never forget my purse, so it isn't so bad." Then, I remembered that the same thing happened to me five years earlier when we drove to Eilat. I forgot my purse and wallet at home. So, I retorted, "Yes, it did happen before, and still, it isn't such a bad thing."

I was surprised by the compassion I had for myself and my forgiveness of the mistake I made.

Then, I looked inward and wondered what was behind that forgetfulness. Although it has happened in the past and I take my purse everywhere almost like the Queen of England, this forgetfulness is very rare.

When we re-examine and analyze things that happen in our lives, we can inspect them from several perspectives.

We can analyze an event psychologically, based on the concept of a Freudian slip, and ask why my subconscious chose to leave the purse behind at Ori's. In other words, why did I leave my "baggage" behind but still remembered to take my cell phone, which is the instrument I use to communicate with others, along with my car keys which allows me to move freely?

We can also look at it from a spiritual viewpoint. What is the universe trying to tell me when it allows me to communicate and be mobile, but holds my baggage back? What does it mean that it held back my ability to purchase things and attain the material expression of my desires?

When I analyze my own subconscious, I have a better understanding of myself and the desires and fears that are behind my actions and choices. When I look at the event from the universe's perspective, I understand the bigger picture, and can perhaps even observe things from a bird's eye view. I can look at the paths and journey that the universe is trying to guide me through.

Both those perspectives require compassion, which is derived from eliminating criticism and acceptance of ourselves. I need to step out of my own anger and soar to see things from above, where the clouds can clear away and I can discover my own coastline, allowing me a deeper understanding of my situation. And so, my purse spent the night at a friend's house while I spent the night trying to decipher the meaning of our temporary separation; and it made me happy to see the compassion grow within me.

Welcome to the Portal

of Joy

Welcome to the Portal of Joy

63. Joy is One of the Most Important Emotions

In Judaism, joy is practically a mitzvah, "And thou shalt rejoice in thy feast." "And thou shalt be altogether joyful" (Deuteronomy 16, 14-15). What is important to understand is that the more I succeed in being joyful, the more joy I bring to myself and others. In Hebrew, the words "happiness" and "joy" are used interchangeably, but if you go back to the chapter about happiness, you'll see that joy is only one of the many aspects of happiness.

The most important mitzvah in Hasidic Judaism is to rejoice. I could say, "How can I rejoice? I'm sad." Hasidic Judaism would reply: No, joy is completely in our control. We must rejoice out of an internal decision and not out of circumstances. It's a choice, a technique: You can pretend to be joyful until you actually feel joyful. Fake it till you make it. If you're sad, don't listen to songs that will make you feel blue; instead, watch funny videos about babies and cats and laugh.

This doesn't mean that we are not allowed to be sad – not at all. Sadness, pain, anger, and all other negative emotions have a place in our lives. However, we tend to feel pain and sorrow much longer than we tend to remain in a state of joy. Joy is a significant portal to happiness. Often, we don't allow ourselves to be joyful because we feel uncomfortable when everyone around us is having such a hard time; how can we allow ourselves to rejoice?

But joy is contagious, and it also has great healing powers. Laughter physically cures us. When we smile, we release a hormone called oxytocin, which is one of the cutest hormones. It is called the hormone of love because it makes us feel good and it also makes us feel a connection, a sense of togetherness, and the desire to be together.

The opposite of joy: Surprisingly, anger is the opposite of joy. Joy and anger have a certain energy of life and growth. Anger is expressed by yelling or violence while joy is expressed through laughter, dancing, jumping, and skipping.

Course of action: Smile and laugh. Even if we don't feel well and smile on purpose, our facial muscles transmit to the brain that all is well. The brain begins secreting oxytocin and serotonin, which change our mood. The most important thing is when we're joyful or laugh and even when we fool around, we shouldn't stop ourselves and say, "Come on, be serious;" we should embrace the joy and lightness it brings.

One more important tip: When I'm angry, I try to express my anger through laughter, and it often helps to express the anger in a more efficient way that brings me closer to a solution. I am referring to actual laughter, not sarcasm. Laughter channels energy and changes the narrative I tell myself, making it easier for me to handle my anger.

64. How to Cultivate Buds of Joy

One day, a couple of years ago, I was working on my mother's balcony. The sun was scorching hot. I screwed some nails in the balcony wall and made a staking fence for the butternut squash my mom began to grow a few weeks earlier. I've already told you in the Portal of Acceptance chapter how, at the age of 85, my mom became a butternut squash grower. However, since then she's become unstoppable!

After my mom moved the seedlings into the planters we'd made, the butternut squash thought they were Jack's magical beanstalk and rapidly grew, sending branches and tendrils across the balcony, preventing us from cleaning the balcony with all the vegetation on the floor. So, Mom turned to Odi to think of a solution. My husband, bless his heart, explained the wonderful idea he came up with, gave me the materials, and flew to Miami for work.

And so, I found myself going to my mother's balcony with a mesh roll and wall attachment nails to build the butternut squash project. I cut the metal roll to the size I wanted and hung it on the wall, which for the first time I noticed was covered with small ceramic tiles. I had to hammer the nails into the thin intervals between the tiles, and also make sure that I don't knock my fingers in the process (Lia, I'm sorry, I know you diligently and lovingly work on my nails, but I think one is completely ruined).

Mom walked around me, making sure I won't harm, heaven forbid, any leaf or tendril. At the same time, she lifted them with a soft touch, admiring the size, color, and beauty of the greenish leaves. Excited, she showed me the soft buds, tiny circles of green tassels which my mom – being a biologist – knew to identify for their full potential even in those early stages. She saw the ability they had, though still invisible, to turn into flowers and later into beautiful, orange, and tasty butternut squashes.

We completed the project two hours later. I finished building the stakes fence, and Mom was done watching over me to make sure I wouldn't hurt her beloved plants. We then sat down to rest. In return for my hard work, Mom cooked me a delicious lunch that included all my favorite dishes.

The joy and satisfaction we felt at that time made us feel transcendent, and that's what joy adds to our lives. I'm not a biologist; I don't understand much about plants, but like my mother, I'm a grower. I grow ideas and methods. I identify difficulties and recognize solutions even when they have yet to blossom. I love growing and grooming these solutions until they become techniques that help us improve our lives. Living with joy is a technique that I didn't invent, yet I embrace it even if it occasionally requires hammering a nail or two.

65. Joy is No Trivial Thing

Social gatherings are comforting, as anyone who's been at a shiva knows. Mourning for someone is a hard period during which we lament a loved one who has left us. Then our friends, acquaintances, and family members arrive to console us, and together we reminisce and tell funny stories that happened with the deceased. We cry tears of sadness and longing as well as tears of joy that we shed for who that person was, and we find ourselves a little comforted. In order to understand the importance of social gatherings, remember how hard it was for us to rejoice during the COVID-19 pandemic, when we weren't allowed to hold any social gatherings and meet each other.

Joy is one of the most important emotions in our lives and one of the least appreciated. Every package I receive from my online orders makes me overjoyed, even if it's only my weekly vegetable order. It might make us think that joy is a trivial, mundane thing hence not really important.

But we couldn't be more wrong!

The more we succeed in bringing joy into our lives – whether daily or on special celebrations – the more we enrich our spiritual world with joy, laughter, and the pleasure they bring, the more we'll allow ourselves to experience happiness even in difficult times.

THERE ARE SO MANY TYPES OF JOY

Bursting joy and peaceful joy, simple contentment, laughter, smile, peace, running wild, or a pleasant time spent with loved ones.

Joy takes on many different shapes. And each is a handle to opening this wonderful portal.

66. Joy is Health

Norman Cousins is the man who brought the importance of joy to modern psychology's awareness. I heard of Cousins when I learned medical psychology at Tel Aviv University. When I'm asked what medical psychology is, I answer that it's the western answer to the concept of mind-body in Eastern doctrines. Cousins was exactly that combination.

So, who was Norman Cousins? Was he a doctor, psychologist, or neuroscientist who managed to tell the Western world just how important one's state of mind is to one's health? Not at all.

Cousins was an American journalist who was diagnosed in 1964 with severe arthritis caused by an autoimmune disease. His doctors told him that he had a chance of 1 in 500 to recover. But Cousins had other ideas.

He decided he would laugh himself to health. He started taking large amounts of vitamin C, and watched funny videos that would make him laugh his head off. He discovered that ten minutes of deep laughter substantially alleviated his pain and gave him two straight hours of painless sleep.

Cousins wrote about that experience in his book called *Anatomy of an Illness (As Perceived by the Patient)*. Of course, there were those who disagreed with his conclusions and claimed that he suffered from an acute outbreak of arthritis which spontaneously subsided on its own. Yet, I believe like many others that this spontaneity derived from Cousins' insistence on bringing joy into his life during that difficult period.

Remember, this all happened in 1964, long before our

digital age in which movies are available at the touch of a finger. The movies Cousins watched came in large celluloid wheels which were installed on his own projection machine at home, requiring heavy lifting and determination. Think how easy we have it today; we can simply use Cousins' technique to allow ourselves to laugh and rejoice all the way into a state of health and happiness.

Think for a moment, what do you do to bring joy into your life?

Take a minute to invest in your joy.

67. Living Joyously

Due to social and cultural perceptions, many of us tend to think in terms of: "That's how it should be." Many think that living with a deep sense of "duty" and constantly thinking about difficulties and obstacles is more important than living with joy. The false conception is that seriousness is nobler than joy; that joy is frivolous, while seriousness is, well, how should I put it – serious.

In fact, that was the root of the struggle between the *Misnagdim*, advocates of seriousness, profound learning and self-importance, and Hasidic Judaism, which praised the mitzvahs of joy, as noted in Psalms: "Serve the Lord with gladness; Come before His presence with singing." (100, 2)

I am a descendant of a family of great rabbis who objected to Hasidism (known as Misnagdim). The resistance, this "No way!" courses through my veins, along with "That's how it should be!" My whole life is a struggle against the walls that the "No Way!" and the "how it should be" form around my simple joy of life and around the love and passion I have for life and fun. It is about doing things because I feel like it and not because that is the way things should be.

The more I succeed in shaking off those chains of "what should be" and the more I go with joy's flow in every mundane intersection of my life, the more I smile and laugh and take life – and especially myself – less seriously. As a result, my levels of happiness rise, and my life becomes better and more pleasant.

Think about it: Where do you stifle your own joy because you're expected to accept what "should be?"

68. If You're Joyful and You Know It Clap Your Hands

They sat in front of me at my clinic, and they were angry. Very angry.

He was angry at her for not understanding that he was doing everything he could. She was angry at him because he didn't understand how difficult it was for her. And they were both very mad at me because I didn't stop the pain they were feeling.

"I can't do it. She just won't understand that I can't! It's not like I'm playing around – I'm working. Working hard. I can't leave everything at 5 p.m. and come back home. I can't leave the entire staff in the office and leave. What would I say – that my wife wants me to read my kid a bedtime story? It doesn't work like that. I don't work like that. I actually work."

Her eyes filled with tears. "Is that what you think?

That I play around all day? Do you know how hard it is to spend the whole day alone with our children? *Our* children! Not just mine. Every evening I have to make dinner – alone – get them into the shower – alone – and clean up the house – alone. I can't do it all. Then you come home after it's all over, sit on the couch, and just enjoy your life. You watch TV and then go to bed."

They continued arguing about who had it worse.

I looked at them and thought that they were at this difficult stage in life that most standard families go through: two parents and two, three, or four children. There's plenty of work that needs four pairs of hands, but there are only two people who do it all. Just like that, each one is overworked and feels like they're doing everything. After all, each of them works for two. Naturally, it builds up a lot of anger that isn't necessarily based on facts, and it slowly grows within us.

She was mad because she felt she was doing everything. She did, in fact, work like two people. He was mad for that exact same reason. They were both working really hard, feeling like they were carrying the load alone, and the most annoying thing was that they didn't feel appreciated for it.

Now, according to the Seven Portals method, anger is the opposite of joy. So, I decided to approach it playfully. "Let's imagine that we've brought Mary Poppins to your home," I smilingly suggested. "Let's stop the intolerable seriousness of "what should be" and begin to rejoice in what is. Let's play a little," I smiled at her. We decided what was really important to her and what she could give up on. Does dinner have to be really healthy and nutritious – which takes longer to prepare – or could she simply make something that's only okay and healthy but quick? Something that the kids would be happy to eat, and consequently, be less resistant every evening? We decided to add some fun toys to bath-time and house cleaning to include music they can dance to. We also agreed that sitting together with kids on the sofa while watching a Disney movie or a TV show counted as quality time!

We introduced joy into their afternoon routine.

A month later, they sat smiling in front of me. She enjoyed her new routine. She put on 90s music and felt like she was having a party whenever she and the kids arranged the house. She bought a new Dyson, and they danced while using it in turns, vacuuming everything they spilled, dropped, and stepped on in the afternoon.

When he'd get home and the kids were already in bed, they'd drink a cup of coffee in the living room or a glass of wine on the balcony and tell each other about their day. But, at least once or twice a week, he managed to get home early, simply because he wouldn't give up on taking part in the joy in their home.

69. Judaism Sanctifies Joy

Judaism is an agricultural religion. Holidays and important dates are connected to the seasons and to the agricultural work of every season. For example, Sukkot is the fruit and vegetable harvest holiday; Shavuot is the wheat harvest holiday, and Tu B'shvat is called the Trees' New Year.

But the Jewish calendar is originally lunar. That is, every 29- or 30-day month begins with a new moon and ends with its end. The seasons, which dictate the agricultural conduct, are based on a solar calendar which is a week longer than the lunar calendar.

If we want to celebrate the Jewish holidays according to the Jewish calendar yet still make sure they correlate with the seasons of the year and the agricultural significance of the holiday, we must coordinate the solar and lunar calendars, thus turning the Jewish calendar into a luni-solar calendar. This coordination is created by adding a month to the Jewish calendar every four years. We have a leap year – a year that has thirteen months instead of twelve: One year with two Adar months: Adar I and Adar II.

Just see how clever Judaism is. Adar is the month of joy, as the saying goes: When Adar begins, we increase our joy. During Adar we celebrate Purim, where the only mitzvah is to fool around, be merry, and give presents to one another. It's a holiday of joy and giving! That's the month Judaism chose to duplicate – not a holy month full of holidays like Tishrei or bitter as Heshvan or the month of Matan Torah or Passover. The month Judaism chose to repeat was the month of joy and being whimsical.

Some might say that Adar was chosen to be doubled because it's the sixth month of the year, and so it would seem most practical to double this month. But I'm sticking to my theory. I don't know if there's another religion that commands one to be joyful, nor whether there is a religion that commands people to be whimsical. And yet, Judaism has several mitzvahs that command us to be joyful, yet in Adar the mitzvah is to increase our joy, drink, and be playful. It's so meaningful that the month in which we're expected to increase our joy and not just to be joyful is the month chosen to be celebrated twice every four years.

A Joyful Adar!

70. Vice Versa – What a Clever Concept

We're used to seeing things in a certain pattern which dictates our relation towards matters, and suddenly we see things vice versa. We can turn the horse on its head and allow ourselves to see things differently in a new way.

In Hebrew, this term is known as "venahapochu" which some believe is a grammatical mistake. But I believe that the use of that alleged mistake constitutes the essence of the concept of venahapochu. It allows for a perspective that praises the unusual ridiculous, funny, and nonsensical things.

The experience that made me ponder the concept of venahapochu was an exercise I had to do during my studies. We were given a picture of a horse. We were asked to turn the picture upside down, with the horse's legs up, and then draw a horse from that position. We had to copy the painting upside down. I'm no painter, and I've never drawn a horse before, but looking upside down allowed me to draw the best drawing of a horse I've ever drawn.

That's the power of venahapochu. It allows us, through turning things on their head, to connect to creativity, which is usually buried under patterns that we believe to be realities and facts. Once we turn facts (theoretically) on their head, we allow ourselves to see an alternative reality which hasn't occurred to us beforehand. Looking at things upside down is a great way to connect with joy.

When things stand on their heads, it's funny, and it releases laughter and joy that has been pushed down. When it finally breaks loose, creativity and enjoyment pour out as well as some hidden meaning we were unaware of. The less seriously we take things, the more we can manage to stand on our heads and increase the joy in our life.

71. Eeny, Meeny, Miny, Moe – Joy Beats Worries

According to the kabbalah, our entire existence comes from the maker's desire to shower us with abundance. It's exactly like Esther Hicks' *Source*. Hicks is a spiritual guide and channeler whom I really appreciate and who talks about how we all come from a source that is all good. The source is solely good and abundant. Our role on this earth is to build a strong and stable vessel that can contain the light shining down on us. If our vessel isn't stable enough then problems such as punctures or leaks or diseases might occur.

But once we understand that it's up to us, that we must agree to accept the abundance, that we have to enlarge the vessel with our faith in the infinite goodness, then things will "fall into place."

The expansion of the vessel comes from adhering to joy, sustaining from fear and anxiety, understanding that I'm never alone, and am willing to learn from everything that happens.

Once we see things this way, the vessel expands and stabilizes and small and big things become messages and insights instead of trouble, worries, and anguish.

JOY – THE BIG CHEAT IN THE GAME OF LIFE

The Ecclesiastes wrote: "I concluded that there is nothing better for a person to do than take joy in his activities, that that is his allotted portion." (Psalms 3, 22)

Many think that Ecclesiastes spoke out of despair, out of an intention to clarify that our life here isn't important, because it was all vanity. But I read those words completely differently.

I think, this sentence allows us a glance into quantum physics. That same theory that conceptualizes our life here as a computer game, and suggests that the goal, the way to win the game, is to be joyful regardless what happens to us, because that's our lot. That's the avatar we chose for this game, and joy is like a cheat, but it's also the real, legitimate success. The more we learn to rejoice, the more we'll increase our levels of happiness, regardless the circumstances.

So, what will help you bring joy into your life?

Welcome to the Portal

# of Forgiveness

Welcome to the Portal of Forgiveness

72. Portal of Forgiveness: A Process for Yourself Alone

Entering through the Portal of Forgiveness is a challenging process, yet once achieved it allows a huge increase to our happiness. Forgiveness doesn't mean that whoever did something wrong should not be punished. All it means is that I'm willing to let go of my victimhood when I'm wronged or hurt in some way. The hardest part of forgiveness is relinquishing a grudge or victimhood: two extremely powerful forces which come at a steep price. When I insist on holding onto my "victim status" and refuse to forgive something that has been done to me, I maintain my "victim privileges" sometimes. Forgiveness is difficult because forfeiting this privilege is hard. On the other hand, sometimes I find it hard to forgive because my grudge sustains my boundaries and blocks those who've hurt me from coming near me again.

The opposite of forgiveness: Forgiveness allows us to enter happiness, and what pushes us out of it is resentment, vindictiveness, and victimhood.

Let's talk about vindictiveness. It's related to forgiveness, but it's more active and less self-harming than resentment and victimhood. When I carry grudges and feel victimized, I supposedly benefit from it because woe is me, poor old me, now you need to make it up to me. But the price is that I keep myself in a prison and prevent myself from coming out, perpetually haunted as I am by what had been done to me. Vindictiveness – or revenge – is a step further, because when I feel vindictive, I'm no longer a passive victim; I'm active. Victimhood, in a way, is active too, but it actively maintains a sense of helplessness which is one of the greatest killers of happiness.

Course of action: The secret to forgiveness is not saying to the other person, "Okay, I forgive you." It's telling myself, "I'm not a victim."

True, I've been hurt; true, it was painful. But here I am, and I'm moving on. I'm learning what I can from what happened, but I won't let it define me. Forgiveness is not at all a process between you and the person who hurt you. It is a process that is completely between me, myself, and I.

73. Let Me Tell You What Happened Between What's-His-Name's Mother and Me

Many years ago, when my son Rotem was at daycare, he contracted scarlet fever which Dr. Bader, our pediatrician, described as a brutal disease with a simple treatment. In the past people would die of it, like Beth in the book *Little Women*, but nowadays you take antibiotics and it all goes away.

So, after he stayed a week at home on antibiotics, I brought Rotem back to daycare on Monday morning. About thirty minutes after I'd left him there, I got a call from Anat, his teacher: "Ugh... Omna – sorry – do you have a note from the doctor saying Rotem can come back to daycare?"

No, I didn't have a note. I didn't imagine that after he stayed at home for a week and took medication it would cross someone's mind that he shouldn't be able to go back.

"I'm sorry," Anat said. "**What's-his-name's** mother asked if he had a doctor's note and said she won't agree to his return without the doctor's approval. It's also the Ministry of Education's protocol, so you need to come and take him home until a doctor gives you a note."

So I went back and picked him up, and my heart ached when Rotem asked to stay at daycare and I had to say no. Obviously, **What's-his-name's** mother was canceled in my mind. That's it. She doesn't exist as far as I'm concerned. I will never forgive her!

For fifteen years I would pass by **What's-his-name's** mother and pointedly ignore her.

Every time I saw her, I would feel my insides stiffen and the anger bubble up. I would turn my head and refuse to smile at her, as I always do. I wouldn't say hello or ask how she or **What's-his-name** were.

The years went by, and one day I was picking out fruit at our local grocery store. They had nice fruit on a nice day. Looking up from the apples I saw a familiar face, and in my good spirits I smiled and politely said hello. Then, I froze. I recognized **What's-his-name's** mother and couldn't believe I'd just been so nice to her. **What's-his-name's** mother did believe it, though, and she smiled right back and asked how I was.

Then it struck me like lightning – how stupid I was. For 15 years – *15 actual years* – I'd been so mad at someone who probably didn't even know she'd hurt me. And all that time I'd made myself feel bad every time I saw her. I locked my heart and my anger bubbled up. Why? What for?

Then I understood that forgiving others was the biggest gift I could give myself because it means freeing myself of the hard feelings and letting myself exist in a state of enjoyment and happiness. I'm not doing a favor for those I am forgiving; I'm being kind to myself.

Since then, **What's-his-name's** mother and I are very happy to see each other in the neighborhood every now and then, and we even stop to chat about our thirty-something-year-old kids.

74. Forgiving Others Starts with Forgiving Myself

Sometimes I think forgiveness is the hardest thing to do...

For instance, if the kids at school make fun of my daughter, it's very hard for me to forgive them for hurting her. Or if a good friend of mine organizes a gathering and doesn't invite me, I can easily start resenting her.

Over the years I've come to learn that the very process of forgiving is difficult for me not just because it leads to letting go of grudge and victimhood but because of the self-pointed anger I feel for not watching over myself or my loved ones and enabling the hurtful act.

Here lies the real key: Every process of forgiveness must start with forgiving myself (!). What helps me in this process is *Ho'oponopono*.

It is an ancient Hawaiian practice, created to maintain peace and love within the tribal community.

I learned about this method thanks to my beloved teacher Shulamit Lev-Ari, and very recently I got to expand my knowledge and skill thanks to the local queen of *Ho'oponopono*, Keren Cohen.

So how do we use *Ho'oponopono* to successfully forgive? (I'm so glad you asked).

The system consists of saying four phrases:

I'm sorry.
Please forgive me
Thank you
I love you.

These sentences should be said with what bothers me or what I wish to solve at that moment.

For example, if we're talking about the kids picking on my young daughter at school, I recognize the overwhelming anger and I say:

For the anger I feel: *Please forgive me, I'm sorry, I love you, thank you.*

For not being able to protect my little girl all the time and everywhere: *I'm sorry, please forgive me, I love you, thank you.*

For the great pain in me, stemming from the vast love I have for my daughter: *Thank you, I love you, I'm sorry, please forgive me.*

For the vast love I have for my daughter, and the joy of having such a sweet child: *Thank you, I love you, I'm sorry that it gets hard sometimes; please forgive me for not being able to protect you from everything.*

For the strength my daughter builds up to deal with the world on her own: *Thank you, I love you so much, I'm sorry it sometimes comes at the price of pain; please forgive me – I love you.*

By saying these sentences, I can slowly shift to feeling that beneath all the pain hides a great love: my love for my daughter and her love for me; my love for myself and hers for herself.

Once I can tap into all this love, it's much easier for me to forgive the kids who hurt my daughter because I understand that pain is an inseparable part of life, and I can't protect my daughter all the time; it's more important to let her deal with pain and my role is to give her tools to understand how to do so. I understand that I hurt, too, because I love her so much that I feel her pain as if it were my own, but my pain stands for a great love. And, if I focus on love, it's much easier to forgive first to myself for not being able to prevent everything – and then the others who offended me or my loved ones.

75. Why Do We Find It So Hard to Forgive?

There are a couple of reasons why forgiving is so hard:

First, we wrongly think that forgiving is like accepting

that what was done to us is okay, and that's really hard. We think that if we forgive, we're giving up our right to be angry or to claim that what happened was wrong, unfair, inconsiderate, violent, or anything else that it really was. We often interpret forgiveness as saying that the person who hurt us was in the right. But that really isn't the case. Forgiving doesn't mean that I think what was done was fair or right – it really doesn't. Forgiving means I'm not holding a grudge; I will no longer be poisoning myself just because of something someone else did to me. Forgiving doesn't mean it was okay – not at all. It just means that I understand people sometimes hurt one another. Someone hurt me and now it's in the past. I'm moving on. I won't burrow into my pain and live it as if it were my present. This leads us to the second reason: the power of victimhood.

You might ask me, "Hang on, what power does the victim have? What on Earth do you mean by 'power in victimhood?' After all, the victim is mostly powerless against what was done to them." So, yes, the victim does experience powerlessness; but – and this is a big but – when I view myself as a victim, I don't need to take any responsibility for what happened or for what is happening right now. For example, *my life is terrible because my parents beat me and I'm 50 years old and it still hurts.* Okay, there's no doubt that it's wrong that your parents abused you, but does it justify your abuse of your own children? That is to say, as a parent I might erase my responsibility for my present bad behavior because I see myself as a victim of my parents' behavior. Or if I hurt my partner or my friend and they constantly use this incident to guilt me into giving more than I want within our relationship, again the offended party uses their victimhood to receive treatment their partner might not otherwise want to give. Notwithstanding the reality of being a victim, this means that our victimhood sometimes carries benefits and that by forgiving we might actually have to let go.

Another reason not to forgive is that forgiving means we can't protect ourselves from the offending party; because if we've forgiven them, it must mean that we need to go back to being in touch with them. If the offending party is someone in my life like a friend, a loved one, or a family member, sometimes I link forgiveness to renewing the close relationship. That might seem scary, because when we're close to someone, it's easier to get hurt. In other words, not forgiving builds a wall between me and the person who hurt me, and that's how I protect myself from them. It can be emotional closeness too – not just physical. By not forgiving I avoid getting emotionally close to the person who hurt me, and I block them from supposedly hurting me again. However, this is also a misconception. Forgiveness doesn't mean that I need to resume our relationship or any emotional or physical closeness. I can understand that whoever hurt me did something wrong and I can forgive them without getting back in touch with them. Instead, I just let go of my resentment against them and the victimhood I've been carrying after they had hurt me.

76. Is Revenge a Dish Best Served Cold?

Another reason we don't forgive is because we're

unwilling to let go of revenge; because sometimes it's our strongest driving force in life. When someone hurts us, it makes us feel powerless, and powerlessness is one of the hardest emotions to feel. When I'm angry and I want revenge, it gets me out of the powerless feeling and helps me feel capable. Forgiving inherently means letting go of revenge, and that's scary because it could make me feel powerless again; if I haven't gotten my revenge and I let go of it I'm powerless, incapable, and weak.

So, what does it mean when people say that revenge is a dish best served cold?

After all, when a dish leaves the kitchen, it's supposed to be warm but it gets cold if you wait. What it means is that you need to take time to plan a worthy revenge and that it takes patience to achieve it. If you ask me, however, revenge is a dish best taken off the menu, because it does you more harm than good.

I do want to emphasize that revenge or thinking about it *is* a force that can help get us out of a powerless state, because thinking about what we'll do to someone who's wronged us helps us reconnect to our chi – our life energy. I don't have to carry it out later, but it *is* something that can help me get out of my state of helplessness. When I start to plan my revenge, I get on the path away from helplessness. Revenge is the inverse of forgiveness, but it's more active and less detrimental than grudges and victimhood. When I carry a grudge and feel like a victim, I supposedly benefit from it because now someone needs to compensate me. But the price is that I keep myself in a prison that I cannot escape, perpetually carrying what was done to me.

Forgiveness is the hardest portal for most modern western cultures to connect with. Once I understood the beauty of forgiveness, it propelled me forward. But our lifelong education is completely opposed to it. American culture frames the avenger as a good Hollywood hero and revenge as a meaningful act. This culture makes it hard for us to give up on revenge and victimhood. In Israel where I've lived most of my life, we were raised with Jewish culture which dictates that we deserve things for being victims; we were persecuted and we must never forgive and never forget. It's ingrained in the Jewish-Israeli ethos. The Arab culture has a vendetta principle including murder for familial honor. It is a lack of forgiveness profound enough to claim lives. But when I manage to forgive – to let go of both revenge and victimhood; let go of the "woe is me" attitude – I can be much happier.

77. Not Forgiving is a Form of Power

Some people are unwilling to forgive because it gives them power over others. Sometimes this becomes their core psychological mechanism, even if nobody has actually hurt them. Some people, for example, are nicknamed "energy-suckers." It's not a professional term, but it's a term that mental healthcare professionals occasionally use among themselves. Those energy-suckers (or narcissist as they are often referred to) are very manipulative; they constantly control people through guilt trips and, as anyone who grew up with a

Jewish mother (if not by religion, then Jewish in spirit) knows – guilt is a powerful tool.

Those people have techniques for creating guilt. For example, they tend to present themselves as unfortunate and poor, framing every request or claim against them as behavior stemming from unexplained personal hatred that they have nothing to do with. Another technique is to take general statements and treat them as though they were directed against them. Then, the energy-sucker can prove their misfortune, because everyone exclusively chastises and dislikes them. Some use this behavior to allow themselves to behave in certain ways that they wouldn't have tolerated from others. For example, they might crudely insult people and then say: "Sorry – I'm just being honest. I'm not a hypocrite like you." Once again, they activate the mechanism of guilt ingrained in all of us and accuse us of not reaching their "honesty levels." They say offensive things and then claim with feigned naivety: "I was just joking. Don't you have a sense of humor?" The person they're talking to is left, yet again, feeling guilty because *it was just a joke, just kidding*. But if you try joking with those energy-suckers, you'll see exactly who *doesn't* have a sense of humor.

Energy-suckers also tend to think everyone is against them because they're sure everyone is bad-mouthing everyone else behind their backs. Why is that? Because that's what they tend to do. They try to pick fights and turn people against each other, so their manipulations work better. Because they don't know any other mode of social engagement, they're convinced that everyone else does it too.

It's important to stress that energy-suckers aren't born evil. In most cases, they develop all the mechanisms I've described at a young age as a way to deal with a harshly critical, compassionless environment that always blamed them for their and others' mistakes. They're not worse people than us; it's just that their only source of power as kids was the deflection of responsibility through guilting their environment, and they continue to employ this mechanism out of a lack of awareness.

Energy-suckers refuse to forgive, even when nobody hurts them, because forgiving means letting go of the power they gain from victimhood. Why am I elaborating on this? For two reasons:

First, to help those who are being manipulated by guilt to recognize their situation as such, in order to allow themselves to refuse to keep going along with this tedious technique.

Second, sometimes these techniques of manipulating others through guilt are so deeply ingrained in us that we do it without noticing; once we become aware of these things we can try and make the educated decision and learn to forgive in order to become happier people instead of keeping up such behaviors.

78. So Why Should We Forgive?

Dr. Gabor Maté, a globally-renowned expert in trauma and addiction, asserts that trauma is not what is happening to us right now, but what is happening within us as a result of what happened to us in the past. And that's the good news, as this is where forgiveness comes in. I can't change what has already happened to me; the event that caused the trauma, but I can change what I experience inside. By managing to forgive, I transform how I experience what happened. Forgiveness, then, is a trauma-healing process; by choosing not to forgive, I'm practically choosing to keep experiencing the trauma.

Sometimes people tell me: "But this is completely unforgivable." So, it's important to stress again that forgiving doesn't mean that what happened is okay or that it doesn't really hurt or that no harm was done. Forgiving, actually, is self-care. Because the grudge I'm holding onto keeps me tethered to someone I don't want to be tethered to, by forgiving someone who has hurt or wronged me I actually free myself of their influence. In other cases, by not forgiving I keep myself hurt, hurting, and wronged, and keep myself from allowing myself to move on and enjoy the present. I'm stuck in the past, and instead of breaking free of the painful event I continually experience it as though it were present and not in the past.

79. Forgiveness will Set you Free

There's nothing more liberating than forgiveness.

And I'm not just talking about forgiving myself, which is of course the most freeing thing in the world. It's all about inhibiting my self-deprecation over every mistake I make or every poorly-thought-through deed, stopping my self-flagellation over every failure, or every time I hurt others. Forgiving myself is like firing a personal assistant who is always there to constantly blame and pester me; it's extremely liberating.

But I'm talking about frankly and genuinely forgiving those who have actually hurt me.

Yes, letting go of various wrongs, injustices, and heartaches that I can rely on when I need to feel miserable and sorry for myself.

Actually forgive; because forgiving means understanding that the past can be changed.

Forgiving is changing the story of what happened and how I got hurt, or more accurately how others hurt me. This story is not easy to change, because it's an old tale that has been with us longer than most of our friends. Who would I be without the stories about the pain I suffered through harm and insult?

But there's nothing more freeing than letting go of those stories.

It's a genuinely transcendent feeling. The willingness to forgive others is the greatest gift I can give myself. And I intend to reward myself with that, because it's in my hands.

80. Who's the Hardest to Forgive?

Since the early 2000s, we've seen many studies demonstrating the close connection between health and forgiveness. We know that a traumatic state causes cardiovascular reactions such as heightened blood pressure and accelerated heart rate. The sooner we regain our initial cardiovascular state, the less damage our health will sustain. Every injury creates a state of stress, and that reaction creates an allostatic load on the body. The allostatic load is the wear of the body, building up over time when we are exposed to recurring or chronic stress. It represents the physiological consequences of prolonged exposure to fluctuating or heightened nervous or neuroendocrinal reactions, stemming from the recurring (fluctuating) or chronic (heightened) experience of stress. The more I manage to forgive, the more I lighten my allostatic load and increase my immune system's capacity. In the courses I teach at **HappinesSkool**, I teach various techniques to help us forgive.

Studies show that forgiveness reduces stress levels after the experience of a traumatic event and also reduces intrusive thoughts that tend to recreate the trauma, thus lowering the allostatic load and helping improve our health. But apparently when a daycare teacher, for instance, says to one of the children: "Forgive them now," it has fewer health benefits than if she were to say: "You go to the same daycare every day; you'll both have a nicer time if you can forgive each other." Why is that?

Studies on the benefits of forgiveness show that forgiveness out of a perceived lack of an alternative – *we have to keep working together* – actually results in more stress and impaired health. Contextual forgiveness, on the other hand, which stems from the understanding that it's the forgiver's best course of action, results in even greater health benefits than those whose forgiveness is merely a default character trait. As in every other portal, the process of forgiveness needs to be internal and intentional; a lack of alternatives is the greatest hindrance to experiencing happiness and, as it turns out, enjoying physical health as well.

Can you guess whom we find it hardest to forgive?

That's right: our mothers and our fathers. People who participated in the study and had been hurt by their parents struggled to forgive them the most, even when forgivingness was one of the participants' personality traits.

Evidently, our absolute dependency on our parents as babies or young children makes us experience their offense as unforgivable.

81. Yesterday, I Was Darn Sure I Was Right

Yesterday I felt like I was doing everything for everyone and that nobody even noticed me: Like I was running around and making things and fetching things, and my needs were pushed to the back of the line as if they were even in line at all. In short: I felt like nobody even took me into account.

I ran through all these scenarios in my head about how I was so (right) and how I am this (right) and they weren't at all or in any way (right), and I felt hurt, miserable, and deeply offended. So very offended.

At this point, I just wanted to hurt them back. I wanted revenge like in an '80s Clint Eastwood Z-movie: *They did this and that and all sorts of things to him, and now he's out for revenge.*

I was running through these scenarios where I just up and left, and they would regret not appreciating me while I was around because now they'd lost me and everything I'd done for them.

Then I decided to take a shower, set off on my vendetta all nice and clean, and stood in the shower under the pleasant water. Slowly the fog lifted and my mind asked, "And how will you feel?"

"Like shit," I answered.

"And is it worth it?"

"Of course. As long as they suffer for everything they've done to me and how they've made me feel."

"Okay," my mind answered, far wiser than I was at that point. "Let's talk for a second about the seven portals to happiness. What portal would you recommend that someone use to assist in such a situation?"

Hmm, now it had my attention. "Maybe compassion? No, probably forgiveness: to let go of grudges and agree to let go of victimhood."

"Good. And then what?"

"Love. It's obvious: Remember the great love I feel and receive; try to feel it and tap into it in spite of being insulted and angry."

Then I got out of the shower and put off my vendetta. Instead, I decided to open the matter for discussion with love and forgiveness, and the results delighted me immensely – and not just me.

Lions and Tigers and Love

of My!

Lions and Tigers and Love, Oh My!

82. What is the Opposite of Love?

If you were to ask a little girl what the opposite of love was, her answer would have probably been "hate." But the truth is that the opposite of love is fear. Love is a positive feeling we strive for, and the more love we have in life the more happiness we will experience. This sometimes applies to giving love even more than receiving it. When we love and are loved a feeling of safety envelops us. But at certain points in our life when we feel no love – inwardly or outwardly – fear creeps in. A long list of difficult feelings can add on to that fear, like hate, anger, and resentment. If we closely examine negative feelings we've experienced, we'll often find that fear was their underlying basis. For example, when someone cuts me off in traffic, I get scared, but my reaction is often anger.

Unconditional love – directed both at myself and at the world – will always negate hate that is directed both at myself and others. When my tanks of love are full, there is no room for fear, and without fear, hate is neutralized.

As Osho said: "Life begins where fear ends."

83. What's Fear Got to Do, Got to Do with it?

When I wrote my book, Carmel, my editor, asked me, "What's fear got to do with it? It's not a portal, and it doesn't really bring happiness, does it?"

So, the answer is: Yes, and that's exactly why. Not only does fear not bring happiness: It drives happiness away. And, like every threat, to understand how to handle it, we first need to look it in the eyes.

Fear is a biological instinct that's there to protect us and ensure our continued existence. We are neurologically wired to fear, because it keeps us from jumping off the edge of that cliff or running straight into the tiger's mouth. So fear as an emotion has its reasons and place in the purpose of keeping us alive. The problem starts when there are no tigers around, and we get addicted to the feelings that fear awakens in us because, as those who are addicted to horror movies know, fear releases addictive substances in our bodies.

Because fear has a vital biological reason for its existence, it's hard and even dangerous to let go of it completely. But, in our modern surroundings, where mortal danger is reduced, very often fear becomes worry. Worry means living in a bad future that might never actually happen.

And what does happiness have to do with all of this?

Because of its biological importance, fear is at the base of our emotional scale, and many of our negative feelings are a result of fear. But, most importantly, fear is the opposite of love, because when I am full of fear, I fail to feel loved, and I won't allow myself to love others. This is how fear fills my inner tanks, leaving no room for love in my heart. And, because love is a massive portal to happiness, when I'm afraid I have no way to experience happiness through love.

Moreover, fear is the foundation to all portal inversions. When I'm afraid of being unloved I appease and don't give; when I'm afraid of not having enough I take instead of accepting. If I'm afraid of not belonging I criticize instead of being compassionate. If I'm afraid of being hurt again, I do not forgive. That's how fear distances us from all portals of happiness.

This is why it's important to talk about fear: Where fear rules, happiness eludes us.

84. Faith Drives Away Fear

I'm a woman of faith. Deep faith. And this makes me dauntless. I believe in the goodness of the universe, and in the good in each and every one of us.

I feel that we're all from the same source and that we embody that source, like waves in the ocean. I believe reality happens to us, but how we respond to it and how we interpret it and engage with it matters far more than the reality we experience.

People go through horrible things and emerge stronger and sometimes even happier while others struggle to handle a most pleasant reality. It's not reality that determines how content we'll be in life; it's our outlook that does.

Let's be frank: We not only don't understand most of what happens in the world, our senses cannot even comprehend everything.

We can be at the heart of an event and be unaware of 98% of what's going on around us because our brain filters out what our senses transmit and tosses away most of the information.

Yet we have the gall and arrogance to say, "If I don't see it, it doesn't exist."

So, hello; I'm Omna, and I've decided to rid myself of the need to believe only in what I see or hear.

I've decided to give up on the need for tangible evidence of things I know in my heart to be true. I've decided to consciously allow a much more profound, expansive, massive and magical world than my mind can currently comprehend to envelope me and exit around me. Ever since I've made this decision, my life and world have constantly improved.

I invite you to join me and deepen your understanding of the complex, wondrous world we live in; to stop being afraid of believing and to understand that the proof we're asking for is so often simply irrelevant because who can measure love or see it? Is that a good enough reason to deny its existence?

85. Worrying: Shield or Burden?

Very often, parents who worry about their children's risk-taking come to see me at my clinic. It's most common with parents of teenagers, who have gotten their driver's licenses, go out until late at night, or want to try out skydiving or mountain climbing. It often involves behaviors perceived as risky and dangerous to the teenager and to others around them. So why are we so inclined to take risks?

The main appeal of risk-taking is that it moves us forward. We evolve, grow, and develop only when we leave our comfort zones. Leaving our comfort zones is always a risk. A crawling baby wants to walk; when they walk, they want to run. This need to move forward, from safely and motionlessly lying to trying to roll over, sit, and walk, is ingrained in our very biological humanity. It's a biological need – an impulse, even – to take yourself somewhere you haven't gone before. But, without moderation, this need which moves us forward so well is dangerous. If we follow the risk without inhibitions, we have a good chance of falling off the cliff. This is where fear comes to our aid.

Fear is our risk-management mechanism. Similar to the need for risks, fear is also a biological mechanism. It's not always easy for us to know what animals feel, but a scared animal exhibits its fear clearly and other animals recognize it. When I feel the need to move forward by taking a risk, fear kicks in to make sure that I'm afraid of getting too close to the edge so I don't fall off the cliff and risk-taking doesn't end my progress.

When our children are young, we as parents can create a safe environment for them, where their need for developmental risk-taking is controlled. But as our children grow, we have less and less control over their environment and consequently over the risk levels in their lives.

That's where worry comes in. Worrying is our way of

feeling protective over our loved ones. If I worry, I'm a responsible parent watching over my kid. But does endless worry – worry that doesn't let us sleep at night and is often the basis of arguments with our kids or loved ones – really protect them, or does it simply exhaust both us and our loved ones instead of creating the safe space we strive to achieve?

86. Does Someone Have Something to Gain from Our Fears?

The story of the storm that didn't happen is an excellent example of how fear is used to manipulate us.

I don't consume media, particularly not the news, but the storm set to arrive one winter weekend a couple of months ago was hard to miss. People kept talking about it; events were canceled because of it, insurance companies sent out worrying text messages, and everyone – everyone – panicked and tried to control their sustained damages in advance.

Then came along Thursday: The sun shone, the sky was a radiant light blue, and not a single thing stirred. It got a bit windy in the late afternoon, and everyone waited with a mix of fear and anticipation: Here, the drama's about to start up. Yet, apart from a few drops of rain and an afterthought of wind, nothing happened. Half-shut windows were all the protection you would need.

I want to note that I don't believe in irresponsibly ignoring the weather or the price that comes with ignoring clear and present dangers, but the story of the storm that didn't come is a wonderful example of how the media inspires pointless panic because panic sells.

It sells news broadcasts; it sells commercials; it sells protective gear which turns out to be unnecessary, and it inspires a primordial fear that helps sell anything as long as it's well-presented.

WHEN FEAR TAKES OVER

Some days I look around and ask myself: Well... now what?

It's important on such days to breathe in deep and not fall into the pits of fear, and instead to remember that everything is made of moments, that there are always options, and that, as my beloved husband says: "The good guys win at the end."

Even if the end looks far away, even imaginary, I stick to my values: love, acceptance, compassion, giving. And I know that the end will be good, because if these are our values – the good is already here with us.

87. Must We Live in Fear of Lack?

Almost thirty years ago, in Louise Hay's wonderful book **You Can Heal Your Life**, I read about the idea that every tomato holds enough seeds to grow more than a hundred tomato bushes with each growing dozens of tomatoes and each holding enough seeds... and so on.

This morning, during a chat with my good friend Rabbi Ayala Samuels, I remembered this wonderful adage.

Our world is a world of abundance, where one tomato, one grain of wheat, or one woman can produce many tomatoes, grains, or people. Yet for some reason so many people live in a mindset of lack, fear of shortage, and physical, emotional, or spiritual hunger stemming from this fear of present insufficiency and worry about future insufficiency; feelings that won't allow us to experience the elementary abundance in our world.

I think that when I can internalize the notion of abundance, I can bring this abundance into my life. Abundance doesn't just refer to money. Money is part of it, because it's an energy of abundance, but it's also friendship, family, community, celebration, a roof over my head, food for satiation, and most of all a feeling of belonging, safety, and love. The more I know to recognize where I belong and feel safe, the more I can love and allow myself to be loved. The more grateful I can be for all of these things, and live on the side of abundance and of appreciation of all there is, the more that abundance will come to me.

If you ask me, it works.

88. Shall What I Dread Come Upon Me? (Job 3:25)

Job is a successful man: A rich lord and baron who suddenly finds himself struck down and robbed of everything he has. How does he respond to this shower of disasters that befalls him? He claims that this is what he had feared all along: "What I dreaded has come upon me."

What makes a rich, strong, healthy, successful man fear the loss of his property, family, and health? Why would Job worry that the horrible disasters God casts on him will come to him?

The more things we have that we love and desire the higher the risk is of losing those things or people. When we focus on the loss or fear of loss, we increase the odds of that loss figuring into the reality we experience.

Just as a pregnant woman notices many other pregnant women around her and just as the road is packed with the same car we'd just bought; our focus constructs the reality around us. When we focus on worrying about what might happen to us, we find ourselves in a reality consisting of those worries, and there it is: What I have dreaded shall come upon me.

89. And What Matters Most is to Know No Fear at All

Over the past few years, as part of my happiness research and the founding of the HappinesSkool, I've been making substantial changes in my life. I've been going about this process by changing my mindset and forging new beliefs that serve me far better than my old beliefs. Saying that it's a process of the past few years might be oversimplifying things because if I think about it hard, I started on this path when I was 16 years old and decided to start smiling at people and greet them happily and loudly. Since that point I've gone through years of introspection and self-knowledge through academic degrees, extensive psychotherapy, and the understanding of many other people in the clinic and the people I hold near and dear.

So it might be more accurate to say that over the past few years this process has gained sharp momentum and has been accelerating thanks to some amazing women I've met along the way, who have taught me new things. It is also thanks to international mentors who have explained how things work and with which I took digital courses and in-person workshops all over the world. And of course, thanks to my academic research in the field of happiness studies; because once a nerd, always a nerd, and what a nerd loves most is to study.

Recently I took part in a course on how to run a crowdfunding campaign in order to publish the book you are currently reading. As part of the course, we were asked to think of an inspirational phrase that guides us. I realized that the phrase guiding me was Rabbi Nachman from Breslav's words: "What matters most is to know no fear at all." That's the whole Torah on one foot; or, rather, the second foot along with "Love thy neighbor as thyself."

These two phrases signify our life's whole emotional range and the right way to handle it.

As my Odi once told me, many, many years ago, "In order to love your neighbor as thyself you need first to love thyself." Thus, all of life's studies manifest in Rabbi Akiva's wonderful quote because it teaches us to love both our neighbors and ourselves. Rabbi Nachman's wonderful phrase "and what matters most is to know no fear at all" is a lovely complement because if we let no fear enter negative feelings will have no basis on which to squat within us.

Welcome to the Portal

of Love

Welcome to the Portal of Love

90. The Portal of Love is the Master Portal to Happiness

Why is love a master portal?

Pure love contains all other portals within it. When we love we are grateful; we give gladly, we're willing to devote ourselves and trust, we see humanness in others, and are inclined not to criticize as much. We find it easier to forgive when we come from a place of love, and love fills us with joy. This is all true, of course, when love is free of fear. But what does fear have to do with love?

The opposite of love: We enter happiness through love, and the opposite of love is fear, as explained in the previous chapter. Fear is an emotion that lies beneath many other negative emotions such as hate, anger, and revenge. When we love and feel loved it reduces the levels of fear within us. The more love we have in our life, the less room there is for fear to enter. Fear is a weakening emotion, thus the less we fear, the happier we get.

Course of action: Love. See the beauty and not the ugliness in the world around us. We should let ourselves get excited about the small things in life like puppies or babies. Allow ourselves to love and not fear being disappointed or getting hurt because we will obviously be disappointed or get hurt at some point. It's an inseparable part of life. But if I won't allow myself to feel love because of that fear I'll be losing something great even before anything disappointing or hurtful happens. The clever thing to do is to allow ourselves to feel the good things and reduce our fear of the bad things that could happen.

91. When Was the Last Time You Asked for a Hug?

Last Friday I was itching for a confrontation. Actually, it started the day before. I felt everyone was annoying me, including the people I love or just strangers, but also the saleswomen in the supermarket, other drivers on the road, someone I talked to on the phone, my mother, and most of all Odi, my love.

Oh man, I was so pissed.

Now, I already know when I'm looking for a fight, but it isn't always helpful. Especially if I have no control over what is genuinely upsetting me.

So, on Thursday I went to sleep frowning, but still in control. On Friday morning, however, I opened my eyes and felt the lava that boiled and bubbled inside of me the other day about to burst. Every breath, movement, and word made me want to blow smoke or bite.

At some point, quite early to my delight, I managed to stop and tell myself, "I don't want to feel that way. I don't want a day of insults, frictions, and muttering of cynical remarks under my breath."

I turned to my love and told him: "I suggest you hug me."

"What?" he asked, momentarily surprised.

"I suggest you hug me."

Gladly, he accepted my offer and hugged me, and it was really all I needed: a loving hug.

That moment I felt the steam leaving me the same way it does when I open a pressure cooker. From that moment onwards we really did have a peaceful weekend.

Why am I telling you this story?

Because this is exactly what I teach in this book. That's the way through the Seven Portals of Happiness: understanding our own hidden motivations and learning to receive that hug that we really want. Every time I realize how to use it in life, it deeply moves me, and I just have to share it.

92. Is Your Family Nuclear or Granular?

When Noam went to Amit Daycare he came back home one day, a few days before Family Day, and explained to us that we're his granular family because we're his parents and siblings. Since then, I started saying granular family instead of nuclear family, because the concept fascinated me. But today I understand why I liked the idea of a "granular family."

A nuclear family comes from the capitalistic-patriarchal concept of a father and a mother and their (preferably biological) children. It is a small unit, meant to be an independent unit. It is a unit that is a nucleus, the closest and hardest part to crack in an atom or in a kernel of a fruit. It is the part from which, if possible, new sprouts will grow and perhaps even the next tree, but only under specific conditions and certain constellations. The economy, statistics, cultural conceptions, and modern patriarchy are all based on this unit. But if we turn the nuclear into granular it becomes a whole different story.

Take a pomegranate for example. There's a phrase in Hebrew, "full as a pomegranate" that translates into "full to the brim." It is an expression related to the pomegranate's grains and refers to wealth, abundance, and multiple possibilities. If we think of our family as granular and not nuclear, we'll understand that the **modern family** – that interesting concept that grew in western culture in the last decades and is gaining momentum worldwide – is a concept which allows us to see familyhood as a pomegranate. We're all grains in a pomegranate, and the different family compositions are an expression of abundance in and of itself.

A granular family can be made of parents and children from first, second, and third marriages. It can include several generations which are connected by genetics and/or love. Granular parents can be of the same sex and granular parenting can be performed by several people who were married to the same person in different time periods. In short, it refers to an abundance of infinite possibilities of love connections that make up granular families.

Like wiser people have said before me: "Out of the mouth of babes and sucklings hast thou found strength." (Psalms 8, 3)

93. Can You Love Too Much?

One of my greatest flaws is that I really love American pop music from the 50s. It's sweet music, consisting mostly of corny love stories that comfort my heart. Earlier today, I happened to listen to the song "I love you much too much" by Alma Cogan, and started wondering to myself: What does it mean to love too much?

I mean, I believe that love makes the world go round, and love is the most important emotion. So how can one love too much?

If love is the most empowering, elevating emotion – whether you love or are being loved – why do we feel sometimes that we love too much?

When I feel that I love too much I actually feel helpless, and that is the hardest feeling to experience. Why?

When I love someone or something, the love itself makes me vulnerable because what or who I love can be taken away from me. It could be a partner who might leave me, some object or property I might lose, or a parent who passed away. Thus it was "taken" from me, so to speak.

Since the fear of losing who or what I love is the fear of losing love itself or the feeling of being loved, one may conclude that this fear derives from feeling that who and what I am is not enough and that I need to work hard to be loved. It is as if the love I receive depends on something. It can be my behavior or presents that I'm expected to give, or any kind of giving that doesn't come from my desire to influence love, but rather from my fear of not getting the love I want to get. And that's why the "I love too much" feeling is truly an expression of the feeling of "I'm not good enough the way I am," and "I should work harder to receive love."

Did you ever feel that way? If so, what did you do about it?

94. Does Unconditional Love Exist?

For me, the portal of love is best represented by Shavuot.

Shavuot is a Jewish holiday that actually celebrates love – a holiday of unconditional love. This love exists both in the Mount Sinai Revelation of the Torah and in the book of Ruth which is read during Shavuot. When Moses presents the written Torah to the Jewish people, everyone answers, "We will do, and we will be obedient." The acceptance of the Torah is presented as unconditional.

No one, not even one person, said: "Tell us what it says, and we'll think about it." No one said: "Give us a few days to consider." The acceptance was absolute and unconditional. It's like when a baby is born and we give one look at that magical creature that had just come into the world and we know without a doubt that we'll do everything in our power to make sure they have the best life possible. That's unconditional love and unconditional acceptance regardless of the circumstances.

Ruth the Moabite, the most famous proselyte in the history of the Jewish people, represents unconditional love. She decided to stay with Naomi, her mother-in-law, in a state of poverty and uncertainty out of sheer love. "And Ruth said: 'Entreat me not to leave thee, and to return from following after thee; for whither thou goest, I will go; and where thou lodgest, I will lodge;

thy people shall be my people, and thy God my God.'" (Ruth 1, 16) We learn that this unconditional love brings to Ruth both honorable Boaz's love and the respect of being the mother of the dynasty of Jesse and King David, which is the highest of honors in Jewish tradition.

How is it for you? What is unconditional love for you? Do you agree that bringing it into our lives brings us happiness?

95. Try to Act from Love

One of the most restricting aspects of human society is the policing of our own bodies.

For instance, society dictates what should or shouldn't be covered, what's the right or wrong skin color, and what's too big or too small. It changes from one period to the next, in different places and cultures. As we can learn from the story of Tamar, the wife of Erl in the biblical days, whores would cover themselves in head and face coverings, while decent women would reveal their faces.

I believe that one of the most liberating things in life is the decision to take back agency over our bodies and decide for ourselves what to expose, what to wear or what not to wear, and when and where to wear it. For example, I've worked as a nude model for painters, and the levels of freedom and liberation that occupation has given to me are priceless.

Self-love means, first and foremost, to accept ourselves with love at every size, color or hairiness, and not constantly try to change ourselves according to the model of beauty that others have decided that we should follow. I'm not ruling out any fashion, makeup, or any other cosmetic product, as long as the makeup, the mani-pedi, or any other fashion thingy or procedure come from a place of joy and amusement. Then, those things are a blessing.

I'm not against changing one's looks. I'm against the self-hatred that is very often attached to these changes.

96. Free Inside – Little Moments of Grace

When I made doughnuts during Hanukkah earlier this year, I kept thinking how much I would have wanted my brother, Yehonatan, to try them, and what a pity it was that we didn't celebrate many Hanukkahs together over the years because I lived in Israel and he lived in North America.

Recently, I've been thinking about one of Yehonatan's hand gestures; a funny movement that he'd do when he'd snatch something from the plate that I just took off the stove or that was waiting to be served on the counter – this circular movement, that swiftly takes something that was not actually served yet, a kind of rotation straight into his mouth which ends with licking his fingers, since he used them instead of a fork. Even now, as I write down the description of that movement as I see it in my mind, my eyes fill with tears.

When we lose someone we love, whether they pass away or are lost in any other way, we miss even the things that used to make us upset about the person. It could be little things like leaving things out of place or insisting on doing something in a specific way.

So now, when I really miss Yehonatan's circular hand movement and I remember how I used to reprimand him when he'd take something from the plate before it was served, I remind myself of how important it is to be aware of this in the here and now; when the event is actually happening.

And this year, when the kids came to "steal" some jelly doughnuts before I even put jelly in them, I knew to look at them with loving eyes and remind myself of how blessed I was for having people that I love who can annoy me on a daily basis.

97. Crying is Power

The French philosopher, Michel Foucault, claimed that knowledge is power. Knowledge for him is the representation of the age of information. He believed that whoever holds the management and distribution of information is in control.

On the same note, I claim that crying is power. Crying allows us to feel our emotions in the deepest, most profound way to the point of giving physical and material expression to these feelings. That is the power of the next age, the age of love, empathy and connection, whose technological representation is the internet.

The modern age was the age of rationalism and information. Gender-wise, you could describe it as the age of modern masculinity. The postmodern age, the one we've all stepped into in the last decades, the one that our children's generation was already born into, is a totally different era.

There's a reason that social media leads this age. Technology, developed through centuries of science and verbal communication, has built the platforms which allow us to connect beyond oceans and continents around the globe. Verbal communication, the queen of logic, slowly made room for visual communication which was marginalized and underappreciated but now takes its much-deserved place again at the center of human communication.

Visual communication is 100% emotional communication. It triggers our emotions and makes us feel them. The strongest expression of emotional communication is crying. Babies who can't talk, communicate with their loved ones through crying. Studies show that crying stimulates physiological emotions of empathy, love, willingness to give, to protect, and connect.[7]

The ability to cry, an ability which only exists in the human species, and that in many patriarchal societies is associated only with girls and women, is a huge emotional strength to the crier. It releases oxytocin, also called the hormone of love, which is a substance that makes a powerful emotional connection between people. It actually affects everyone in the surroundings of the person who is crying by connecting everyone through the same physiological mechanism in a very powerful and emotional way.

No doubt that generating empathy through crying has been misused for over thousands of years, mainly

7. Bylsma., L.M. (2019) The neurobiology of human crying. Clinical Autonomic Research.

because crying was the main strength of disadvantaged groups. But in the current age, when technology is used to create a pan-human connection, it's about time crying gets its well-deserved place and finally be acknowledged as an incredible human ability of connection and love.

98. The Happiness in Longing

Fresh fragrances, a playful breeze, and gorgeous blossoms that begin to brighten my backyard are all signs that spring is coming along with Passover, the holiday of freedom. What a wonderful idea it is to celebrate liberation from slavery. In a way, we're all enslaved by our everyday routine. Having to wake up early again and pack lunch. I've been doing this for a quarter of a century. That's as slavery as routine modern living gets.

So, this week, our youngest child went on a school trip. Suddenly, I didn't have to get up and make his lunch, and I could just arrange my schedule without having to take into consideration where Noam needs to be or making sure he gets there.

I won't lie – the sense of freedom that I felt on that first day made the concept of Passover "from slavery to liberation" all the clearer to me.

I made appointments far from home, according to my own schedule. I drove off without thinking who might need my help and for what. I felt as free as a sparrow.

On the second day I was still euphoric. Odi was on a long flight, our older children already lived in their own apartments, and I, like a teen whose parents were away for the weekend, enjoyed the complete freedom of "alone time" and nothing more.

But in the evening of the second day, I began thinking of loneliness. I tried to understand what kind of life I would have had if this were my daily routine: drive wherever I want to go whenever I want to, meet people, and constantly do only what I want to do, and I suddenly realized I was overwhelmed with a sense of longing. Don't get me wrong, I really love that feeling of missing or longing. Missing people or experiences is a central part of my life, and I do have a lot so I have what to miss.

Of all the days, on the day that I didn't have to wake up and pack lunch or take care in one way or another of the people I love, I understood how this responsibility that allegedly ties me down is the basis from which I can go out to the world and conquer it. It's like a string tied to a helium balloon that is me, allowing me to fly away without getting lost.

Like Kris Kristofferson says: "Freedom's just another word for nothing left to lose."

Indeed, that utter freedom, which many times we crave, means giving up all the anchors tying us to our lives and are the same anchors which enable us to peacefully float, knowing that we won't fly away to oblivion. Love is one of these important anchors, if not the most important one.

P.S.

I know that some might say the line I quoted above belongs to the legendary Janis Joplin. True, Janis did spread this line, but Kris wrote it down and performed it first.

99. Love is Exponential

Love is the most meaningful power in our lives and on earth in general.

When we are in love the world becomes magical. But there's the catch: That same loved person has the power to take all this magic away from us; let's say, if they leave us. On the other hand, if we fall in love with ourselves that power stays ours.

Most people might think that falling in love with themselves is self-centered and vain. But self-love is basically to do unto ourselves what we do when we fall for another person. When we fall in love, we project onto our loved ones the qualities we love and appreciate and the qualities we'd want to have in our lives. They don't always have these qualities, but we believe that they do and that's the reason we're in love with them.

On the other hand, self-love means adding these qualities to our lives without depending on anyone. Characteristics like generosity, giving, warmth, and appreciation are things that if we direct at ourselves will make our lives a personal ongoing honeymoon. It doesn't mean that there won't be a time and place for other loves and loved ones; not at all. In fact, it's quite the opposite. As every parent knows, when a new child arrives, the love for the older child doesn't lessen but grows because love brings love.

And that is the foundation of the portal of love.

And Now

What Portals are
Your Strength

And Now, What Portals are Your Strengths?

Questionnaire

You've come a long way since filling out the questionnaire at the beginning of this book.

Has anything in your approach to life changed following your reading?

Do you feel differently about any of the Portals?

Fill out the following questionnaire (identical to the questionnaire at the beginning of the book) and examine how your answers have changed.

So What *Habit of Happy* Have I gained?

QUESTION	Answer number 1 or 2	Sum of the points of each portal
When I hear the word "no" or when things don't happen my way, I: 1. Get upset and try to do everything I can in order for things to happen just the way I want them to. 2. I try to understand why things aren't happening my way, and look for other ways to find a solution.		**The Portal of Acceptance**
When I receive a present, the most important thing is: 1. Having a gift receipt, in case I want to exchange the present. 2. Someone thought about me, and wanted to make me happy.		
When I give a present, the most important thing is: 1. I've given what was expected of me, and my present is worthy and appreciated. 2. I make sure I have thought about the person receiving the present.		**The Portal of Giving**
When I see someone who's dressing well or someone who has done something great, I: 1. Wonder to myself whether they're better than me. 2. Love to compliment them and make them feel good.		
When someone has made a mistake, the most important thing is: 1. Explaining to them why it's a mistake, what they've done wrong, and where else they've made that mistake. 2. Helping them realize that we all make mistakes and it's a part of life.		**The Portal of Compassion**

If I've scheduled a meeting with someone and they're running late, I'll think: 1. Why is it so hard to be on time? 2. It can happen to anyone; we're only human.		
When I see a pretty flower or enjoy a delicious cookie: 1. It doesn't have any impact on me, it's just another part of life. 2. My heart swells with joy, and I feel very lucky.		**The Portal of Gratitude**
When something good happens to me or when someone helps me, I: 1. Believe that it's a given; this is the way things are meant to be. 2. Tell everyone, am thankful, and make sure to express it.		
When I'm sad, I tend to: 1. Remember and think about sad things that happened to me and others. 2. Allow myself to feel sad, but make sure not to lose myself in that feeling.		**The Portal of Joy**
When I watch TV, I'd rather watch: 1. News, scary dramas, TV series, exposes, or documentaries about injustices and corruption. 2. Funny TV shows, amusing video clips, science, or nature documentaries.		
When someone hurts my feelings I: 1. Will always hold it against them, think about it, and feel that life is unjust. 2. I won't think about it much. If necessary, I'll keep my distance so I won't get hurt again.		**The Portal of Forgiveness**

When I think about the mistakes my parents have made, it's clear to me that: 1. They've really screwed me over, and some things cannot be forgiven. 2. Every parent makes mistakes, and usually, they make those mistakes unintentionally and not because they don't love us.		
When I love someone, the most important thing is: 1. They think about me, they notice what I care about, and they give me attention. 2. To have fun together, do something together, and find things that we can enjoy together.		
Love to me is: 1. A privilege that only some get to enjoy; it's often painful and makes me feel vulnerable. 2. The most important and therapeutic thing on this earth.		**The Portal of Love**

Now, add up all the points in each portal separately.

Results

2 points at a certain portal – There's plenty to work on. You don't use this portal often in your life. However, by exercising daily, it could become one of your happiness portals.

3 points at a certain portal – Great, this is a portal that can open the door to more happiness. Practicing can turn it into one of your strong portals.

4 points at a certain portal – Congratulations! This portal is one of your strengths on your path of happiness. This portal is dominant in your life, and serves as an anchor on your daily happiness journey.

To Finish on a Sweet Note

Traveling to the Edge of the World for Love

To Finish on a Sweet Note: Traveling to the Edge of the World for Love

Odi and I have been together for almost forty years, and sometimes I think this love is my most important fuel for life. Odi's father would ask me, "Where do you get the strength to do everything you're doing?" And I would answer: "My husband loves me," and we would both laugh happily. But that love almost eluded me. What happened, as it happened, was this:

Many, many years ago Odi and I lived in a tiny house with a huge backyard in a nice suburb, very close to the beach. We were both studying in university and had been living together for two years. Every summer Odi would fly to Alaska and work aboard fishing boats to earn his keep for the coming school year. I worked as a flight attendant for an airline. I would fly back and forth throughout the year, and study for exams at the big Fifth Avenue branch of the New York Public Library. Along came summer, bringing with it the end of our third year of university and the end of our studies. The question of "Where to next?" hung in the air between us; when I brought it up, Odi announced that he was going to Alaska because John Quinn, the owner of the fishing boat, had sent him a one-way ticket and he did not know when he would be back. I filled my flight schedule and went back and forth like there was no tomorrow and the summer would never end. But it did end, and my airline flight season ended with it. I was granted a wildly discounted ticket for my first holiday flight; my friend Ayelet offered me to join her on a dreamy vacation to the Philippines, but my heart whispered, "Speak with Odi," and that's how I got the idea to fly to Alaska.

***

And thus, I embarked on a five-day journey, flying and sleeping on airport benches, from Tel Aviv to Los Angeles, from Los Angeles to Anchorage, Alaska, and from there to Dutch Harbor, a small island at the edge of the world, somewhere between Alaska and Russia. I had the name of the fishing boat and John's address in Seattle. I got his home phone number, a wall-mounted landline somewhere out in Seattle, from the international switchboard.

When I landed in Anchorage, I called John and asked him to tell Odi I'd be there very soon. He stuttered for a bit and was really shocked, one might even say frightened. He made sure three times that he had understood correctly and that I was really in Anchorage on my way to Dutch Harbor, there at the edge of the world, and then explained twice more that he didn't really know when the boat would make it back to shore, because they had been in the middle of a fishing expedition for the past twenty-five days, but that he would relay the message. That was the first time it occurred to me that I might end up making this whole trip without actually getting to see Odi.

When I landed on the island, the airport arrivals hall was about the size of my parents' living room back home, and, no – their living room wasn't all that big. The luggage carousel had to be driven by a manual lever, and the ten passengers I shared the tiny airplane with all vanished at lightning speed, each heading off in their own direction. I stood there lost for a moment, then approached the sole help desk in the hall where the clerks directed me to the only motel on the island. I settled in and then, like many adventurers before me, set off to discover the Island I'd found myself on.

Mid-October, Alaskan fall as cold as Israel in mid-winter. Beautiful lakes and mountains, with daylight lasting until nine in the evening. I found a small café by the Delta Dock, where I met Luisa from Mexico who moved to Alaska with her beloved and made the most delicious doughnuts every morning. Like every business in Dutch Harbor, she, too, had had a two-way radio with which one could reach out to the boats that had gone out to sea. Every morning I would stop by her café for coffee and a doughnut, and try to call Odi's boat.

"This is Omna calling the Polar Mist. Come in, Polar Mist."

But there was no response beyond the gurgling static. I walked around the island for three days, going from one radio transmitter to another, trying to reach Odi's boat, but to no avail.

On the late afternoon of the third day, I got back to the small motel after wandering the island. Jack the cab driver from Phoenix, Arizona and John the fisherman from Seattle sat in the lobby together, playing cards and drinking beer. They both already knew I had come from Israel to see my fisherman boyfriend, and they had wished me luck. Newman the receptionist called out to me.

"Hey, Omna, you have a message from the Polar Mist."

"Really?"

"Yeah. They'll be docking at the Delta Dock in two hours."

Time stretched like bubblegum. At six o'clock Jack went on his taxi shift, and I waited another half an hour to get to the Delta Dock, but you couldn't find the boat there if your life depended on it. I approached a group of people standing on the platform and tried to figure out what's what, but they were unfamiliar with the polar mist and they were certain that it didn't dock there. Tears choked my throat, despair climbed up the back of my neck. Am I going to fail having tried so hard and come so far? Am I not going to find Odi? The rain that started to fall affirmed my own rain, and my tears mixed with the raindrops as I stood there and looked at the expanses of ocean from the dock.

A taxi sounded, and a car pulled up next to me. Jack opened his window and asked: "What's going on? Come in, get in the car. At least you won't get wet." I sat in the taxi and started telling him what happened; my voice choked when suddenly the taxi radio started crackling and a familiar voice emerged from it:

"This is Odi calling the Polar Mist. Come in, Polar Mist."

"Excuse me, Jack, can I please use the radio?"

"Of course."

"This is Omna calling Odi. Come in, Odi."

"Where are you? Stay where you are. I'll be right there."

I crane my head near the window and try to see through the rain. I want you to get here already!

Suddenly I think I see a familiar figure around the corner. I leap out of the car, not caring a single bit about the rain or the looks of the people hanging around on the platform. Yep, that's Odi there by Luisa's café. I start running and I see him look at me and start running toward me. We run for seconds, we run for years, and suddenly his arms wrap around me. I feel my feet detaching from the ground. I cling onto him through the layered coats that wrap around us both, just hoping I'd never have to let go. The world turns and turns again, and I don't know if this wonderful dizziness is because I'm being turned in midair or because of the hormones my brain is pumping into my bloodstream. I'm flying.

A FIFTEEN-YEAR JOURNEY ENDS HERE, AS I WRITE THESE LINES

And maybe it is not really the end, because the whole purpose of the research, the model that I've developed and this book, is to give you tools to enhance happiness and make it more easily-accessible in your everyday life.

So… which portal was your favorite? And which demanded more effort to get through?

What insight provoked the most thought? Which tools have you already taken up while reading?

Thank you for getting this far and choosing to make The Habit of Happy part of your life.

***

If you've still got a taste for more, and want to expand your knowledge, I invite you to visit the HappinesSkool: a digital academy for a good, happy life.

https://www.doctorosher.com/

Made in the USA
Monee, IL
03 November 2024

69225588R00128